Internet Mergers and Acquisitions

A Collection of Articles From My 20+ Years in the Lower Middle Market M&A World

Michael Eric Furlow

Copyright © 2020 Michael Eric Furlow

All Rights Reserved

All rights reserved. No part of this book may be reproduced in any form or by any electronic or mechanical means, including information storage and retrieval systems, without written permission from the author, except for the use of brief quotations in a book review. Any questions about the book, rights licensing, or to contact the author, please email:

eric@furlowconsulting.com

The information provided within this book is for general informational and educational purposes only. The author makes no representations or warranties, express or implied, about the completeness, accuracy, reliability, suitability or availability with respect to the information, products, services, or related graphics contained in this book for any purpose. Any use of this information is at your own risk.

Cover background by Darwin Bulos

www.furlowconsulting.com

First Edition

ISBN: 979-8629278269

Table of Contents

Preface 1
1 Two very different "7 times annual EBITDA" company valuation multiple scenarios 3
2 The most ruthless tactic in private mergers and acquisitions 7
3 Digital Agency M&A: Buyside Assignment, Valuation and Liquidity 13
4 "Pre-Revenue" is not always a curse word 25
5 Company Valuations: the reasons, ranges, reliability 27
6 The MSP Company Valuation Dilemma 33
7 The mirage of company valuation multiple expansion 39
8 The perfect number and blend of MSP Services 41
9 Tech Buzzwords from an M&A Perspective 43
10 Why do you think your company is worth that valuation? 45
11 Pros, Cons & Tendencies of financial, strategic and individual business buyers 47
12 7 reasons why M&A transactions don't close 53
13 14 Misconceptions & Mistakes with Company Divestitures 57
14 Software developers and architects … "If you build it, they will come." 71
15 It's nice to meet you but you're an "outsider" 75
16 When there is no doubt it's time to sell your company 77
17 Why billion-dollar companies acquire tiny million-dollar companies everyday 79
18 A perfectly overpriced, initial "business asking price" 83
19 Never do business with this person 89
20 There are 4 company valuations for every Internet service company 93
21 Business liquidity/desirability scoring system 97
22 Losing your job due to a tech merger or acquisition. 105

23 The startup strategy "pivot" ... there is a hidden cost 111
24 First discuss the geographic layout of the Internet service business with its owner 115
25 There is a better question to ask the business owner than, "Why do you want to sell your company?" 119
26 Positive thoughts for startups raising capital 121
27 2 types of business sellers ... proud and desperate 123
28 7 things to do 13 months prior to selling your Internet service company 127
29 The difficulties of selling a 50/50 equity partnership 131

Preface

For almost 25 years, I have been an independent mergers and acquisitions consultant specializing in the Internet industry. I have focused on providing two professional services. First, I help business owners and CEO's organize, market and sell their Internet service companies (AKA "the sell side"). Second, I have been retained by over 150 financial and strategic buyers around the world helping them locate, analyze and acquire various Internet-related assets and companies (AKA "the buy side). I have been involved in over 250 transactions for clients in more than 30 countries, finding buyers and sellers in all sorts of tricky situations and learning many lessons along the way.

This book is a collection of articles I have written over the years, articles that provide valuable information about many aspects of mergers, acquisitions and divestitures in the ever-evolving Internet industry.

ONE

Two very different "7 times annual EBITDA" company valuation multiple scenarios

Once many IT industry company valuations have passed their peak, it is difficult for many business owners to extract more value from their company than the declining industry valuation multiple is taking away ... so if you are going to sell your Internet service company, it is better to be too early than too late.

Over the last 20+ years, I have worked in many recurring revenue business model IT industries such as wireless telecom, long distance service, SMR, ISP, CLEC, SaaS, MSP's, VAR's, web hosting and now cloud services ... and close to the same thing happens over and over. The specific industry valuations rise, peak, then start to decline. This is no different than many other industries, however the evolution typically occurs much faster in IT industries.

No one needs to read an article to learn that the best time to sell their company is at the peak valuation, however it is well worth understanding the increased cost of being late even if the same "7 times annual EBITDA" company valuation multiple can be received. This market timing is very different than the scenario of selling a common stock for the same price either before or after the valuation peak. For example selling a stock at $60 before it peaks at $75, or selling it after the peak when it declines to $60. There is not a penalty for selling after the peak ... the seller receives the same $60 all cash at closing.

A few comments on "selling at the peak"

Most people can't pick the exact peak of any market ... at least not on a regular basis, especially the valuation peak of an Internet industry with so much bias noise coming from all of the information sources either trying to boost the value or bring it down. And sellers shouldn't feel inept if they don't pick the exact peak because even the best Wall Street traders admit they can't pick the top or bottom of specific markets or individual stocks on a regular basis. We have all heard the expression "if you can pick 60% of an upward or downward move you have done well". The truth is picking a 60% move is more impressive than it appears because the trader first has to pick the right direction, up or down.

So back to the business owner in the IT space.

If a business owner sells before the peak of the industry valuation, maybe at 7 times annual EBITDA, he might miss the valuation run up from 7 times to 9 times but he will almost always be in better financial shape than the business owner who sold at 7 times after valuation multiples decreased from 9 times back to 7 times ... for the following reasons.

1. One of the reasons industry valuation multiples decline is because revenue growth prospects decline. When and after this occurs EBITDA margins typically decrease as both acquisition cost per customer rises and average revenue per customer declines as more and more businesses

compete on price alone. So if the same "7 times annual EBITDA" valuation multiple is being applied to the new lower EBITDA figure, the total proceeds of the sale will be less.

2. There are fewer buyers when industry valuation multiples start to decline, so this typically equates to less attractive deal structures buyers are willing to offer. For example, as an industry is rising buyers might have to pay 75-95% in cash at closing yet as industry revenue becomes flat deal structures become less attractive for sellers, maybe 50-75% down ... and of course when industry revenue declines the deal structures become even worse for sellers, maybe 25% down and payments over time (sometimes post-closing payments are based on future customer retention).

So the post peak "7 times EBITDA valuation" can involve a lower total sales price, and the net proceeds being spread out over many months, if not a couple of years.

If an owner realizes he missed the peak industry valuation, the best thing to do might just be to 'eat-it' and sell the company (if pivoting the company is not possible or desired), because odds are valuations will not get better. What I have seen many owners do is agree to sell their company today only if a buyer is willing to give them last year's higher valuation multiple... which they will not get, so they keep the company. The following year they really want to sell, yet they again want the prior year valuation multiple ... which they will not get, so they keep the company. This is a common story.

Ending on a happy note:

There is nothing evil, embarrassing or irrational about staying in a declining value industry. I have seen plenty of business owners knowingly and happily ride industries down because they loved the business, predicted the downturn early on, cared for the employees, and figured out a way to make a profit all the way down ... some owners making very inexpensive and well-structured company acquisitions along the way.

TWO

The most ruthless tactic in private mergers and acquisitions

Buying and selling a private Internet service company can be a smooth process which evolves into a win-win for both the business buyer and the business seller ... OR it can turn out to be a disaster where either the shady seller misrepresented the company or the shady buyer went into the deal fully intending to bait and switch the seller.

One thing which makes me angrier than anything else in this profession is when a business buyer takes advantage of a business seller. Buyers can do this in a number of ways but the specific way I am referring to is called a "bait and switch"... a silly name yet ruthless tactic.

This is how it plays out ...

After a buyer and seller have agreed to the terms of a deal and signed a Letter of Intent, they start working on due diligence and the purchase agreement. One to two weeks before closing the unscrupulous buyer says the following to the seller.

> "I am so sorry to tell you this but our board of directors has grown cold on this deal because (insert lies) and no longer wants to pursue it. We discussed this dilemma for days and decided that we would still be

willing to close this deal next week if you would agree to a price reduction of 15%. We realize how disappointing this news must be and if you decide not to accept this price reduction and walk away from the deal, we will totally understand."

It is true that some buyers discover things during financial, operational, legal, and technical due diligence which were either not revealed or were misrepresented by the seller, so a proposed reduction in price is absolutely warranted. In these situations not only is the seller lucky the buyer is still willing to close the deal, but the seller probably expected this price reduction was coming.

However, some buyers fully intend to do this to sellers before they ever sign the Letter of Intent.

Why? ... because they know that some sellers, after grumbling, complaining, cursing and debating ... will say "ok".

Why? ... for two reasons ... first, because the seller is days away from no longer having to manage employees, vendors, and customers. Second, because the seller has already spent the money in their mind ... paying off debt, paying off the house, paying for college for all the kids, taking care of relatives and finally pursuing the hobby they have been dreaming about for years. <u>The fact that all of these dreams could disappear in the next 24 hours if they themselves don't simply say "ok", is predictably insurmountable for many sellers. And buyers know this.</u>

One of the many great things about the Internet is, it's now a small world and word travels fast in professional communities. Buyers simply cannot do this to sellers over and over without becoming known for this type of tactic. I actually have a list of people known to pursue this tactic as a strategy. For many years I have swapped names of these shady characters with other M&A professionals in the US, Canada, UK and Australia.

There are a few ways to reduce the chance of this happening and to lessen the adverse effect if it does happen.

1. **Avoid buyers who have a reputation for doing this.**

    Sellers should network around their industry and ask previous sellers how their deal went. Chances are that if a buyer did this to them they will be more than happy to reveal the details of their divestiture experience.

2. **Before a LOI is signed, try to reveal as much as possible to the buyer so there is the least amount of additional education required post LOI.**

    Of course many times the customer list, software code and certain agreements are just too proprietary to reveal to buyers pre-LOI.

3. **When an LOI is signed, the seller should make the expiration a short window so if the buyer doesn't close the deal the seller can go back to the #2,3,4 buyers, sooner rather than later.**

4. **Right before a LOI is signed, the seller should make a follow up information package and send it to the #2,3,4 buyers, so when the seller signs the LOI with buyer #1 and can no longer**

> communicate with the #2,3,4 buyers ... they are as educated as possible, so if the deal with the #1 buyer doesn't close, the other buyers are that much closer to closing the deal.

Side Note about sellers getting deposits as a form of protection:

I guarantee that in most seller's initial Company Information Package provided to the buyers, which includes trailing three years financials, legal, operational and technical details, there is at least one error in them. All the buyer has to do is say ... "If there is a misrepresentation in the information I was given prior to the signing of the Letter of Intent, I can walk from the deal and get my deposit back." <u>So it makes the deposit a waste of time. Negotiating the terms and conditions of a deposit can be extremely time consuming, taking focus off the actual deal. In addition a tiny deposit doesn't work either because in a $5mm deal a $10k deposit will not have any bearing on either party's decision. So the bait and switch mentioned above still works with a $10k deposit.</u>

In closing I feel I must add a few positive comments defending the typical business buyer.

Many business buyers (maybe not "most") are very honest and just don't want to get ripped off by a seller misrepresenting the company. During due diligence buyers discover things about the company that the seller initially was either hiding or not presenting in the clearest of light in fear that the buyer wouldn't want the company. This happens all the time. So what do buyers do, they either walk from the deal or suggest a lower price ... rightfully so. <u>In anticipation of this, many buyers price some due diligence disappointments into</u>

the LOI valuation, then if during due diligence none arise, they got a better deal than they thought. However, if they do find a skeleton or two, they can still close the deal with the original LOI pricing and deal structure.

In addition to discovering misrepresentations during due diligence, the business environment can change in 2-4 months and/or the buyer's strategy can change as well. So it is reasonable for a buyer to change their mind about a deal within the 2-4 months a deal is being worked on. It happens.

But we all know it doesn't happen over and over with the same buyers.

THREE

Digital Agency M&A: Buyside Assignment, Valuation and Liquidity

I have been assisting individuals and CEOs acquire, divest and value Internet service companies since the days of the dial-up modem, so to witness the "Digital Agency" industry evolve from basic website design and old school advertising to where it is today has been a fascinating journey for many of us.

My 2018 six-month buyside consulting assignment

In mid-2018 I was approached by the CEO of a software development agency in the northeast US. He wanted to entertain acquiring a few digital agencies to both scale up and diversify his company's offerings. My role was to assist with the strategy, identify the pool of target companies, contact then educate each target, schedule and participate in conference calls, collect initial due diligence info, and help pro/con each target.

I am approached with this type of assignment at least 2-3 times per month and only end up accepting about 2-3 per year. Why do I only accept 2-3 of these assignments per year?

- I end up spending an enormous amount of time with each buyside client, so the personality match has to be close to perfect.

- I need to be impressed with the CEO, their company and their acquisition strategy.

- It is far more financially lucrative for me to only represent sellers.

- Many buyers never end up acquiring a single company.

So why did I take on this assignment?

- I was and still am very impressed with this CEO and his company.

- Sometimes during the evolution of specific industries, they explode with regards to the speed of strategic change of the industry participants. This has certainly been the case with the "Digital Agency Space" … and there is no better way to learn exactly what is happening than to have conference calls and 100's of due diligence information exchanges with CEOs who are entertaining selling their Digital Agencies.

The History of Digital Agencies

How did we get to this point? There were several industries which were growing and evolving by themselves … think

Old School

- Advertising: branding, package/product design, print, PR, media planning & buying (established 100+ years ago)

- Cell phones (established around 1990+-)

- Technical infrastructure: data centers, fiber, wireless, satellite (established in the mid 1900's)

- Websites: design and hosting (established in the mid 1990's)

New School

- Software Development: mobile app, wearables, IoT, AI, BI, custom software, blockchain, application testing-management-support, etc.

- Visuals: UX/UI, AR/VR, graphic design, audio-video production

- Marketing: Social media, mobile ad, email, PPC, SEO/SEM, content

- Managed Services Providers: Cloud services, IaaS, PaaS, cyber security, IAM, network (design-maintenance-monitoring), SaaS (101 flavors) etc.

- The massive eCommerce Universe

- Financial: Cryptocurrencies and the explosion of fintech

(Did you notice how I blended MSPs into the new school of Digital Agencies ... or should it have been the other way around? ... I was surprised at how many digital agencies offer many MSP type services ... and why not.)

What happened over the last 5-15 years is, the old school industries evolved and added many of the new school services mentioned above.

What is the urgent rush now?

To get as much of the Fortune 1000 company's technology spend as possible because these client commitments can last for many years and can be extremely profitable. Once an IT business development person has their client's decision maker's attention, it is smart to lock them into as many services as possible. As we know, once mutually beneficial business relationships get traction, it is hard for an outsider to break in.

The Next School

Of course, the "next school" will always provide us with new products and services to develop and market, but the class which every IT Company CEO is always attending is ... which services, more importantly which blend of services should their company offer. Which services should they develop and manage in-house and which should they outsource or white label from 3rdparty providers ... OR should they stay focused on being experts in 1-2 closely related services and be the provider that other digital agencies and MSPs reach out to.

<u>Back to my six-month buyside assignment and the "discovery" questions we asked many CEOs:</u>

The five core questions we used to get conversations flowing are as follows.

Question 1

"Which of the listed 30 digital agency services accounts for most of your annual revenue? And which service accounts for #2 and #3 of total annual revenue?"

- Most of the time, the answer quickly and clearly defined their company.

- Sometimes this discussion led to who they want to be, what steps they are taking to become that type of agency and the hurdles they are facing to finish the strategy pivot.

- From a business buyer's perspective, it is always comforting to hear CEOs confidently discuss their laser focused strategy ... but this is not always what we heard. We heard many flavors of bad news from quite a few of them. And we actually heard the truth from a few CEOs that this is not what they want to do with their life. Of course, these CEOs who want to leave the digital agency space all together are hoping for a business buyer who wants the CEO to leave post-closing ... and that is not what we wanted.

Question 2

"How much of your client work is performed by your in-house full-time employees vs. how much do you out-source to 3rdparty providers or contractors"?

- A few CEOs told us that they perform close to 100% of the work in-house, but most CEOs told us they outsource a percent of the work ... some more than others.

- The perception from many business buyers is that if the target company outsources 50%+ of their client's work to a third-party development company, then why not acquire the third-party development company ... unless the original goal is to acquire the sales and project management talent at the target company.

- Some CEOs told us they only outsource when they are overloaded with client projects, while other CEOs told us that they always outsource specific services for which they do not have an expert in-house.

- Over the months of asking this question many times and listening to the answers, I think we heard every single pro and con to the "in-house vs. outsource" debate.

Question 3

"What year was the company established, what was the annual revenue for the last year, and in what year did your annual revenue peak?"

- While many companies have grown revenue a bit each year since the company was established, I was actually surprised at how many company's annual revenue peaked in prior years. If the answer was simply that they lost their largest client yet have picked up growth since then ... great. However, if the answer was something else, we dug in a bit more.

Question 4

"How many employees do you currently have"?

- This seems like a simple question with a simple answer ... but the implications are huge. The answer was many times the foundation of who the CEO is. If a business buyer is looking at making acquisitions in the digital agency space, the CEO is the largest variable of a sub 50 employee agency.

- If the answer was 40-50+ employees, this told me that this CEO/owner probably knows how to properly manage people and client projects … and equally as important, wants to and is willing to manage people. This is not an easy skill set to master and maintain year after year. The reality is many business owners can't do it, hence one of the reasons why small businesses stay small.

- Having said that, there are many digital agency owners and owners of 101 other types of businesses who choose to stay the size they are. The business owner enjoys client interaction and the creative side of client projects … and much prefer this overspending 100% of their time managing their employees and performing the same company administrative duties over and over while their employees enjoy client interaction and the creative side. I actually totally understand this. I have worked for myself with no employees since 1996. I would much rather do the client work myself than manage employees.

- The downside of staying small is, these small digital agencies with less than 25+- employees are harder to sell. Why? Because the CEO knows many if not all of the clients. If the CEO leaves the company post acquisition, so will some of the best clients and some of the best employees. This is not just a company acquisition risk; this could also happen with a "merger of equals" causing similar damage to the remaining equity partners and the company's reputation and stability.

- The smaller agencies are considered "lifestyle businesses", and unless they have a notable portion of their annual revenue, which is recurring, they are hard to sell with traditional deal structures. Many times in order to complete an acquisition, the deal structure includes much less of the total deal value paid at closing, and more is paid over time based on revenue targets, AKA "earn-outs", or revenue shares.

Question 5

"How many employees work in the main office; how many are in offices across the US and how many work remote?"

- We heard it all, but from an M&A perspective, most buyers would prefer a cohesive team working from one or two offices.

- We also heard all the valid arguments for remote employees, but it is just not what we were looking for.

Digital Agency Valuation and Liquidity Bullet Points:

- I am not aware of any digital agency "industry standard" valuation formulas, rather it is every buyer for themselves, and it is their responsibility to customize each offer according to the value that the specific deal will bring to their organization. Of course, this sounds like it should be the proper strategy within every industry, but it is not. In other industries, the "valuation gods", dictate that valuation is a certain dollar per subscriber, or for example within 6-8 times annualized EBITDA ... but in the Digital Agency space, valuations are all over the map, but from what I have heard and seen, rarely over 1.5 times annual revenue, unless there is a notable SaaS component or proprietary IP.

- So, should the offers be based on a multiple of operating profit (EBITDA)? Sure, that is one of the variables I use ... however it can be a bit counter intuitive. Since most digital agencies are primarily one-time revenue businesses, their EBITDA ebbs and flows with the size and frequency of client projects. It is simply the nature of the beast.

- Are all 5% EBITDA margin target companies in bad shape, deserving of a low valuation? No ... I want to hear the story. They might be growing so fast that every dollar which comes in is going to increased head count. Maybe the digital agency is 100% focused on ecommerce and most of their work is from May to November ramping up for Christmas ... then almost dead from Jan to April, but the CEO keeps everyone on the payroll waiting for the May-Nov ecommerce season. There are plenty of examples of this.

- Are all 30% EBITDA margin target companies in great shape, deserving of a high valuation? Well, they are in great shape as far as the CEO/owner paying the bills for the next few months, but I am not sure what the 30% margin tells me about the future of the company. Is the CEO/owner intentionally "passing" and not bidding on prospective client projects which would result in a profit margin of less than 30%? OR, has this target company's revenue remained at $4mm per year for many years, and the operation is lean and mean with consistent client work, and the CEO/owner wants to keep his agency at about this $4mm per year level.

- **Side Note:** Regarding recurring revenue business models, in other Internet service industries focused more on the infrastructure side, the industry participating companies are more alike. They are all trying to scale up each month by adding recurring revenue customers. After these companies grow for a few years, there are logical company to company valuation metrics.

- The greater the recurring revenue as a percent of the total annual revenue, the more valuable and liquid the digital agency will be.

- The more services which are developed and managed in house, the more valuable and liquid the digital agency will be.

- If a new client is going to end up being 25%+ of the total annual revenue, yet very profitable … of course the CEO should sign them up. Yet of course this well affect the company valuation and liquidity, but not as much as one would think. This single client risk can be offset by a slightly strung out acquisition deal structure addressing the longevity of the big client.

- Ending on a positive note: Keep in mind digital agencies and consulting shops can pivot quickly without substantial cost. This is in contrast to the infrastructure players who are married to their initial technology commitments for long periods.

In conclusion, is there a perfect blend of digital agency services to offer, is there a perfect headcount, is there a perfect inhouse vs. outsource model? I don't think so. These depend upon the founder, the partners and the team members ... what they are the good at, what they want to do every day for years, and if they can develop and sustain a sales pipeline to make it work.

FOUR

"Pre-Revenue" is not always a curse word

I am approached many times each month by owners of pre-revenue startups. To be honest, I am no different than other M&A professionals in that my first thought is … bummer … because of course we would rather hear, "I want to sell my $20 million in annual revenue company, will you help?" However, my 20+ years in M&A in the Internet service sector has taught me not to immediately <u>read this project its' last rights</u>, rather inquire about a few quick basics which can turn my perception of the potential sell side assignment around.

If the pre-revenue SaaS is focused in one of the latest cutting-edge industries, then it's a plus.

If the pre-revenue SaaS is owned and managed by someone or a group of people with a successful track record of building then selling SaaS projects, then it's a plus.

If the pre-revenue SasS developed all or most of the IP in-house, then it's a plus.

If the owners want to keep a portion of the equity and stay on board … and are actually honest about this, then it's a plus.

We have all heard of pre-revenue startups, mostly SaaS, being sold for large sums of money. In most cases they checked the aforementioned boxes. In reality, most who approach me just check the last 2 boxes, which by themselves are rarely good enough.

FIVE

Company Valuations: the reasons, ranges, reliability

The reasons

There are many reasons that business owners, CEOs, investors, exiting partners, soon to be partners, and lenders need a third party to create a Company Valuation Report.

There are the happy scenarios. For example, business owners want to know how much the company is worth to then decide if they want to go through the divestiture process. Another example is an investor wants a second opinion on a company they are thinking about investing in. This investor may have a realistic perception of value and a logical post-closing investment strategy; however they just want an extra voice to confirm and quantify the strengths and weaknesses.

Then there are the situations where different stakeholders are not getting along. These include partnership fights, divorces, financial defaults with investors and lenders, etc. These disagreements are sometimes mild, for example if three equity partners simply disagree on the value of their company because one of the three partners wants to retire and the other two partners want to buy him out … but other than this difference in opinion, they get along fine. Of course, there are the more severe disagreements where different stakeholders are either suing each other, or about to.

My thoughts on the legal fights regarding value are that if one side hires someone to do a valuation, the other side will simply not agree. Having said that, eventually a valuation or a company divestiture will be forced on the parties. Valuations in contentious situations tend to help if both sides of the fight agree to hire someone, or hire three different firms to do a company valuation and average the three valuation figures etc. In some situations, when a single company valuation is received, one party will quickly approve the results and the other party will eventually approve the results as well, not because they agree with the final valuation figure, rather they believe the valuation difference is less than the legal fees and hassle of a continued multi-year legal fight … so they accept the results and move on.

The ranges of valuation formats

There are many formats of a company valuation. Two of the main reasons for different formats are the cost and the purpose or need of a company valuation. One common format of a valuation in many industries is geared towards lenders who focus heavily on fixed "hard" asset values (however irrelevant this can sometimes be in the Internet service sector especially in the SaaS, development and consulting areas). These company valuation reports can be very in-depth and of course quite expensive. These valuations start with a macro-economic overview, then analyze the entire industry the company is in, then analyze the company, finally value individual assets all the way down to the estimated value of every desktop computer in every office. This format of a company valuation is obviously needed in many scenarios because stakeholders commonly pay $20k, $30k, $40k, and yes over $50k for these types of valuations.

But what if stakeholders of sub $20mm companies simply want to know what the company is worth and what buyers will probably like and not like about their company, if it were properly marketed over the next 3 months. These business owners are already in the industry, so they don't need to pay someone to tell them industry stats which they already know … they just want to know how much money the company could be sold for.

The valuation reports I create are focused on the most probable results of a properly marketed divestiture process. My reports are named, "Company Valuation and Liquidity Analysis Report", and contain an analysis of the many value drivers within most Internet service companies. I include the comments, criticisms and praises that a company owner will almost certainly hear from buyers if they put their company on the market … almost word for word.

I have been focused on acquiring, divesting and valuing Internet service companies since 1996, primarily the recurring revenue business models (hosting, access, MSPs, VARS, SaaS, colo, data center) but secondarily the one-time revenue business models (web/mobile/app/software development, digital agencies and IT consulting). I have stayed away from the hardware sales and domain name sales markets.

I include "Liquidity Analysis" because this process identifies the abundance or lack of liquidity for a specific business model and each of the individual service offerings, and this is one of the main drivers of company value. In addition, in today's Internet service world, most companies offer multiple services to their clients. Some of these services are cutting edge and some have been around for a long time. Each service within a company needs to be analyzed and valued as far as its positive or negative contribution to the entire company valuation.

Side Note: Offering a new "cutting edge" I.T. service is not always a good thing because they tend to be cash burning learning experiences for the providing company ... and continuing to offer an "old school" service is many times far from being a bad thing because many tend to be cash cows and are low maintenance.

In the Internet service sector, value is focused around customers, IP, employees, brand name momentum, and of course revenue, profit, growth ... then hard assets (other than the data center world of course). This is as opposed to other industries like real estate or energy where "hard assets" are #1, followed by the other value drivers in different order.

At the end of my reports, I give valuation ranges depending upon how fast or slow the company would need to be sold, and if the seller has any restrictive deal structure requirements.

Reliability

Keeping this concept short and sweet. There are generalists who will value companies in many industries from restaurants, gas stations, hotels, car dealerships, on and on ... then there are specialists who will only do company valuations in a few closely related industries. I have never figured out why a stakeholder would spend their money to hire a generalist as opposed to a specialist ... unless they are hoping the company valuation will turn out better than what the specialist is likely to produce.

SIX

The MSP Company Valuation Dilemma

Many years ago the tech world was filled with single product and single service companies, think long distance service, local phone, wireless paging, SMR, cable tv, dial up ISPs and a few others. This made company valuations relatively easy. The valuation metrics were based on dollar per subscriber, revenue multiples, EBITDA multiples, free cash flow multiples ... of course with the many adjustments for large fixed assets, debt ratios, growth rates, profit margins etc.

In today's world there are still many single product/service tech companies, but more and more tech companies offer a bundle of services, yet still have a primary core service offering which accounts for a notable amount of their annual revenue.

Managed Service Providers today offer many combinations of the following services:

- A/V (audio and visual services)
- BaaS (backup)
- BI
- Big Data/Analytics

- BPO
- Cloud services
- Connectivity
- Content (creation, distribution, storage etc.)
- Cyber Security
- DaaS (desktops)
- Data Center Services (design, construction, maintenance, monitoring)
- Database (mgt., migration, analytics)
- Dev Ops (dockers, containers)
- Digital Signage
- DRaaS (disaster recovery)
- eCommerce (many services within ecomm)
- eMAR (electronic medication administration record)
- Equipment/hardware lifecycle mgt.
- Fintech (many services within fintech)
- Help desk
- IaaS
- IAM (identity and access mgt.)
- IT Audit

- License mgt.
- Migration (customer and/or data)
- Mobile (app dev, payments, advertising, ecomm)
- Network (design, maintenance, monitoring,
- PaaS
- Satellite
- Software Dev
- Print Mgt. (document mgt.)
- SaaS (the 1,001 flavors of a SaaS)
- Security (facilities, network, data, cyber penetration testing etc.)
- Systems Integration, monitoring
- Unified Communication
- VAR
- Vendor Relationship Mgt.
- VoIP-Hosted PBX
- VPN
- Web (DNS, Domains, Hosting, Design/Dev, SEO, SEM)
- Wireless (system design, maintenance, etc.)

And I probably I missed a few.

Sure, there are pure play SaaS operators and old school VARS, but most companies in the tech service sector today are offering a few of these MSP services. So, is every recurring revenue focused tech company now called a Managed Service Provider? It's starting to look like that. This is not a bad thing or a good thing. It is just the new reality for 1,000's of companies in the US and Canada.

The main reason for this bundled or "a la carte" approach is, once a MSP has the attention of the client company's "decision maker" it is very smart to sell them as many recurring revenue services as possible, AKA: get as much of the client's technology spend as possible ... before one of their competitors does. (and we all know that recurring revenue is the holy grail of company value creation). Once these services are purchased, installed/implemented, taught and operational, many of them are hard to replace with a different vendor. In addition, look at this from a customer's perspective ... do they really want to have 10-12 IT service vendors? ... or closer to 2 or 3.

So, what in the world do we do about company valuation when each MSP is offering a different combination, mix and weight of these services ... hence there might not be a perfect company valuation comparable?

Well, the valuation dilemma is not on the sell side. If a MSP's CEO/owner is selling their company, it's easy ... simply organize the presentation well, proactively market the company to a large pool of target buyers (slightly overpriced of course), then wait for the most interested buyers to grumble about the price and make their best offers. Of course, the process is more detailed than that, but you get it.

The company valuation dilemma is on the buyside (or investment side). If a CEO/owner or an individual investor is acquiring a company or making an investment in one, the valuation challenge can be far more difficult because too many times private company merger and acquisition valuation information is incorrect or misleading.

For example,

- In news releases the total price might have been revealed but the deal structure was not. In a $20mm deal, 75% of the $20mm could have been spread out over 3-5 years. So, was this really a $20mm deal? ... no.

- Or, in what appears to be a very high price paid for a company with $50mm in annual revenue, what the public doesn't know is that a small $20mm data center and associated real estate was included with the deal.

- Or, if the CEO/owner asked other people for valuation information on their deals or deals they heard about ... more times than not, they are not told the compete truth. If you think people exaggerate about their golf scores or how many fish they caught last weekend, you should hear some former owners talk about their past deal information.

In closing, when CEOs/owners are on the buyside they should stay "old school" with discounted cash flow analysis models, and pay special attention to any downward trends with any of their many services. Just because target companies are more complicated than they used to be, doesn't mean the simple foundations of company valuation can't remain the same.

SEVEN

The mirage of company valuation multiple expansion

"Multiple expansion" is an idea around company valuation. The idea is, as a company grows from $1mm in annual revenue to $15mm then $25mm and higher, the company valuation multiple will also increase. Two common company valuation metrics are, a multiple of annual revenue and a multiple of EBITDA. I have been acquiring, divesting and valuing recurring revenue businesses in the Internet space for over 20 years. What I have experienced in the sub $25mm private M&A deal market is valuation multiple expansion is for the most part a mirage, it doesn't exist.

Why?

The major reason is simple. In the well-populated recurring revenue-based Internet service businesses such as MSPs, web hosters, some SaaS providers and the many flavors of cloud service providers, *there are plenty of buyers with $1-3mm in cash on hand for an acquisition. However, there are fewer buyers with $5-10mm in cash on hand for an acquisition, and even fewer buyers with $25mm in cash on hand for an acquisition.*

So, for a $3mm acquisition, since there are many more buyers who are bidding up the value of the deal ... the highest bid ends up being close to or higher than the same revenue/EBITDA multiple as a similar $25mm deal, where there are far less bidders.

In addition, smaller $5mm deals have a very attractive quality that comparable $25mm deals don't ... and that is, the smaller acquisition is far less risky than the larger deal. A common example of this is, if a larger company wants to enter a specific geographic market, maybe expand to the other coast, they can achieve this with either a small acquisition ($5mm) or a larger one ($25mm). Buyers tend to prefer the smaller acquisition even if they have the cash on hand for the $25mm deal ... and these buyers are not alone in their logic. If the acquisition strategy is anything other than to simply add scale, buyers many times tend focus on smaller deals.

In closing, when CEO/owners are talking to me about either selling or continuing to grow their companies, I tell them there are many valid reasons to continue to grow the company from a $5mm company to a $20mm company, but if one of the main reasons is multiple expansion ... scratch it off the list.

EIGHT

The perfect number and blend of MSP Services

There are over 50 individual services a "Managed Service Provider" can offer customers. Many CEOs have asked me ... in order to maximize their company valuation and liquidity is it better to specialize in 3-5 services or try to offer as many services as possible ... and which combination of these services is best.

In my opinion, there isn't a perfect number of services. CEOs should focus on leveraging what their team members are good at, and what fixed assets and IP they own or have unique access to which are a strategic advantage over other MSPs. At some MSPs the senior team members have a common history around SaaS, while others around infrastructure, and others around support business models.

My advice is not to think about the total number or blend of services offered as being either a positive or a negative, rather analyze each service and its contribution to increased customer acquisition, customer quality, customer retention, EBITDA and of course free cash flow. We all know of profitable MSPs which offer 5 or less services, and others which offer more than 20. What tends to happen is the MSP which specializes in just 3-5 services will be a nice strategic fit for other MSPs wanting to add these services to their offering, and the MSP which offers 20+ services will be attractive to larger MSPs wanting to add scale, and of course to the army of financial buyers. <u>One important and comforting reality is, there will always be buyers for profitable and growing recurring revenue businesses regardless how many services they offer.</u>

After having this chat with owners, I tell them if they insist on worrying about something, they can focus on the % of total revenue which is recurring vs. one time. In almost every case the greater the % of total revenue, which is recurring, the more valuable and liquid the company will be. So, in the difficult analysis of adding an additional service to an MSP's total offering, the first big question is … is it one time or recurring revenue. <u>If the answer is "one-time revenue", my thought is … it better be an essential service to lock in recurring revenue customers otherwise it will probably be a drag on valuation, liquidity and perhaps cash flow.</u>

As we know, this topic is way bigger than just a one-page article, so thanks for your patience.

NINE

Tech Buzzwords from an M&A Perspective

When I hear a new technology buzzword I first wonder ...

What is it? Is it a product, a service, a process, or something bigger? How far on the horizon is it?

Will the buzzword become its own industry? Will it become a new way of doing business containing multiple industries like "the cloud"? Or will it just become a single product which attains rapid adoption yet quickly gets folded into Managed Service Providers portfolio of services?

I next think about this new buzzword from an Internet M&A perspective, so three important questions come to mind ...

1. Will this new buzzword evolve into a product, service, or industry with primarily one-time revenue or primarily recurring revenue?

    The reason the one-time revenue vs. recurring revenue question is important to me is simple. Recurring revenue companies tend to be far more valuable, liquid and scalable than one-time revenue companies.

2. Will the future providers of this buzzword be dominated immediately by the billion-dollar

companies? or will it possibly create 100's of small private tech companies scattered throughout the US and Canada?

The reason this question is important is simple. For the last 20+ years, I have specialized in organizing, marketing and divesting private Internet service companies. I welcome new mom and pop Internet products/service industries.

3. Which product, service, and/or industries will the buzzword replace? And of course, how fast and to what degree with this cannibalization occur?

In closing, when a new buzzword first appears on the horizon, many people including the media sit back waiting for industry leaders and acclaimed investors to give it credibility or not. If the "thumbs-up" is given, the buzzword spreads like a virus and within weeks the buzzword is appearing on 100's of company & industry websites, blogs, Twitter, marketing materials, LinkedIn profiles, and even people's resumes! It then becomes time consuming to figure out who is actually on the forefront of development and implementation into the sales channels vs. who is just talking about it.

And as always, the companies and investors with plenty of cash to burn will be first ... yet right beside them will be companies and investors with just enough cash-on-hand to get started.

Then here we go again.

TEN

Why do you think your company is worth that valuation?

I hate that question during conference calls. Why? ... because conference calls should be focused on the educational process ... and valuation debates tend to derail this process.

When a business buyer is looking at a target company, one of their first questions is "What is your asking price?". Of course, this is a fair and logical question. However, when some buyers hear the answer, they will go right back to the seller and ask them "Why do you think your company is worth that valuation?".

Stop and think ...

<u>Is any business buyer actually looking for valuation advice from the business seller?</u> Absolutely not ... rather they are looking to get the seller on the defensive to then beat them up on their valuation logic.

- What ends up happening is, the seller becomes defensive then irritated.

- <u>What never happens is</u>, the seller agrees with the buyer during the valuation debate then lowers their asking price.

Business buyers should debate the company valuation with the seller's M&A consultant or broker outside of conference calls.

Many buyers have not learned that other than a business owner's family, their business is the most important thing in their life … <u>and it's very personal to them</u>. Business buyers should realize this and discuss even the weaknesses of the seller's company with respect and understanding.

Back to the common question … "Why do you think your business is worth that valuation?"

One diplomatic and accurate answer for the hard-core business buyer could be: (of course saying this with a big smile and a happy voice)

"My business is a work of art. It's worth what I think it's worth. If this amount is too far from your valuation, I understand. If there is another aspect of the company you need further clarity on let me know."

<u>The goal of any answer is to keep the situation happy and turn the buyer's focus back towards education, due diligence and preparing their actual offer in writing … and away from trying to prove who is the superior "on the spot" company valuation debater.</u>

In closing, most of the time the seller is NOT applying for a post-closing job with the buyer, rather they are just selling their company and the divestiture process is about professsional documentation and education … not about being a clever fast talker.

ELEVEN

Pros, Cons & Tendencies of financial, strategic and individual business buyers

If you are about to market your Internet service company for sale, whether it is a web hosting, cloud service, etc., you are first going to need to identify the buyer pool and educate them one by one. As you start to speak with buyers, you will realize they fall into one of these categories: financial buyers, strategic buyers or individuals. It is important to know the pros, cons and tendencies of each of these buyer types. Why? ... because if you have two or more buyers who have made similar offers for your company, you need to identify:

- which is more likely to close the deal <u>as originally negotiated.</u>
- which is likely to drag the original closing date out for weeks or months.
- which will likely walk from the deal before closing for reasons which were <u>clear and present before the original offer was made and accepted</u>.

Financial Buyers

Financial buyers often do not have investments in the same industry as the target company they are looking at. However sometimes they do, and are looking to make an add-on acquisition for one of their platform companies. There are a few categories of these groups ... private equity groups, family offices, larger institutional investor groups, and smaller angel groups.

Pros:

Most financial buyers are procedurally savvy about the entire acquisition process and have the capital to close the deal.

Cons:

They are under no pressure at all to make the acquisition. They can very easily "pass" on your deal. This is in contrast to many strategic buyers who are under constant pressure to grow or acquire.

Tendencies:

There is a herd mentality with financial buyers. Many of these groups will chase the same deal, or they will all stay away from it.

There are 1,000's of these groups in the US, Canada and the UK, most looking for the same thing. The bare minimum for the smaller financial type buyers is $5mm USD revenue with $1mm USD EBITDA. I receive several emails per day from these groups looking for deals.

Most financial buyers tend to walk away from a deal at the first sign of any negative with the target company. On the other hand strategic buyers tend to press forward when faced with mild negatives because there are forecasted cost synergies and other benefits of the deal which can offset the mild negatives.

Strategic Buyers

These are buyers who are already operating the same type of business as the target company, or a closely related one.

Pros:

Strategic buyers can:

- realize expense reduction synergies and revenue boosting cross selling opportunities, that most financial buyers cannot.
- combine management/employee talent.
- exploit the target company's sales channels and vendor relationships.
- access specific assets such as the seller's company owned data center or valuable IP.

Cons:

There are not many. Strategic buyers account for most M&A transactions. However, some strategic buyers are less capitalized than they should be given their aggressive presence in the market and this can distract sellers, getting in the way of other buyers who are well capitalized and making similar offers.

Individuals

There are two main variables with individuals as buyers: Are they capitalized and are they experienced. I will look at each of these with a simple hierarchy.

Experience: (best to worst)

1. Buyer has years of experience in the same industry as the target company and has completed acquisitions in this industry.

2. Buyer has years of experience in related IT service industries.

3. Buyer has years of experience owning and managing companies outside of the IT space, but none within the IT space.

4. Buyer has no experience owning or managing companies in any industry ... but somehow has a few million dollars available for a company acquisition and thinks they want to acquire an Internet service company. (I used to smile at this as well, but it actually happens more than you think: inheritance, legal settlements ...)

Capitalized: (best to worst)

1. Individual buyer provides personal investment brokerage or bank account statements showing more than enough cash on hand for the acquisition

2. Individual who has a group of investors ready to "fund the deal".

   Risk: The seller first negotiates a deal with the buyer ... then the buyer goes to their group of investors who tell the buyer to go back to the seller and negotiate a better deal ... or the group of investors will not fund the deal.

3. Individual who thinks they can get a bank loan (even if preapproved by the SBA) for an Internet service company acquisition.

   Risk: There is a small chance of them being able to do this. If the acquisition includes a large fixed asset, such as a data center filled with customers under 2-5-year agreements ... then maybe. However, if the value of the acquisition is far greater than the total value of the fixed assets ... then probably not. Having said that, I know buyers who use SBA loans all the time, but they are rare. I more often see buyers fail to secure loans for acquisitions.

Pros:

The seller is probably speaking with the final decision maker ... AKA: the individual buyer.

Cons:

There is little chance the individual buyer will be able to outbid the strategic buyer. Having said that, if there are no other buyers bidding ... then a seller should go with the individual buyer.

Big Risk: While I did say above that a "pro" is that the individual buyer is the final decision maker, in many cases they are actually not. Individual buyers have different types of advisors such as husbands, wives, attorneys, accountants, and "expert" uncles ... who will all tell them NOT to do the deal. Why do they all tell the buyer this? Because it is risk free advice. None of them want to be the person who suggested that they acquire the company ... then the deal turns out to be a loser and the individual buyer ends up with a company half its original size after a couple of years. **What makes this phenomenon especially risky for the seller is, the interaction with these trusted advisors in the buyer's inner circle tends to happen just a few days before closing, when the buyer is getting nervous and reaches out to these people for advice.**

On the other hand, financial and strategic buyers tend to back out of deals early in the process.

In closing, there are different types of business buyers and knowing the pros, cons and tendencies of each is important because when you have 2 very similar offers from different buyers, you need to know which buyer is more likely to close the deal ... as originally negotiated.

TWELVE

7 reasons why M&A transactions don't close

1. Of course the #1 reason is that sellers ask too much money for their companies, and over the course of the divestiture process they don't lower their asking price enough. Let's not forget that sellers have every right to ask whatever they want for their company.

2. The #2 reason is NOT that the selling company is in a distressed situation or rapidly headed in that direction thus making a transaction difficult. If anything, distressed situations are often easier to acquire because <u>a transaction of some sort WILL occur</u>. What is not initially known is, with whom, for how much, and what the deal terms will be. Rather the #2 reason is the seller's deal structure requirements are never met.

3. The seller's company is too unique, too niche or too large in a given space. Many times an aging technology space. In these situations, there are simply too few buyers, and the buyers who are interested don't have the capital and can't raise it.

4. An insurmountable negative. With some sellers, there is a single big negative issue and there

isn't a buyer who can figure out a way to accept it and work around it. Examples: A pending or existing lawsuit, the single largest customer is 40% of total revenue, non-compete issues, a sticky vendor agreement, government permitting/licensing approvals, etc.

5. Too many small negatives. As buyers start to learn about a seller's company, they list the pros and cons. Of course, there is the attempt to quantify the pros and cons but some of these are intangible, hard to quantify, but there is no doubt these issues belong in the "Con" column. Eventually, the list of individual cons becomes insurmountable.

6. The seller's reputation is shady, so buyers don't trust the proposed transaction … in any form … at any price.

7. The seller's company is too unorganized. Sellers can be honest, hardworking, in a great industry, and operating growing and profitable companies (so it appears) … yet if their due diligence information is too much of a mess or missing, buyers will walk away from the deal. The only way a deal occurs here is if the asking price is dramatically reduced or if the deal structure is heavily stretched towards the buyer … neither of which happens … so the deal doesn't close.

Buyers are paranoid, as they should be. They realize that often the most important piece of due diligence information is the piece they either receive last or never receive.

Common seller statements:

- "We don't have those records."
- "We have never tracked that."
- "We don't know how to gather that information."

These statements were sometimes valid 20 years ago, but today these statements are a much tougher sell because companies are buried with their own operational information (... and there is no shortage of vendors willing to help them gather and organize it.)

In closing, there are many other reasons why M&A deals don't close. Some of the reasons have made me laugh ... eventually, while others are so unbelievable, I rarely tell the stories. Only divorce attorneys, psychiatrists, and prison guards have witnessed similar behavior.

THIRTEEN

14 Misconceptions & Mistakes with Company Divestitures

The divestiture of a business is obviously THE most important transaction of the entire life of the business ... and should be treated as such. Over my 20+ years executing M&A transactions in the Internet service sector, I have seen many of the same mistakes being made, as well as selling CEOs and business owners holding onto the same misconceptions with regards to the company divestiture process.

Misconceptions and Mistakes

1. Speaking to 3 versus 300 potential buyers

A mistake many CEOs make is to communicate a possible divestiture with the easiest 2-3 buyers they can think of, then force a deal. It sounds foolish, but people do this all the time. The two reasons that some CEOs do this are:

- They don't want word to get out into the market that the company is for sale. While I do understand this, there are ways to reduce the probability of too many people finding out about the sale. Of course, there is still a chance someone finds out about the sale and unethically shares this information, but the tradeoff is the difference in total deal value is far greater from auctioning the company to 50-300 buyers than the total deal value attained from forcing a deal to one of just three buyers.

- They don't have the spare hours in the day to allocate to marketing the company to 50-300 prospective buyers.

Another problem with just marketing the company to the easiest three buyers is that experienced buyers will know there is not a professionally run process in place, hence they assume the buyer pool must be very small ... and they will adjust their initial offer and proposed deal structure accordingly.

Imagine a CEO who needs to search for a new Chief Technical Officer or Chief Financial Officer. They shouldn't quickly select someone from a pool of just three candidates they already know, rather they should retain experts in the executive search field and instruct them to (1) identify a pool of prospects (2) communicate the opportunity to them (3) screen the pool for the best and most willing, then (4) try to make a deal. In many cases, anything short of this process is simply careless. So why would the divestiture process, which is the single most important transaction in the history of any company, be handled with any less procedural discipline?

Side Note: There are certain companies where there are only 1-4 capable and logical buyers in the entire world. This is due to government regulations/restrictions, technical commitments and in some cases the massive size and/or location of the company. In these situations, the vast buyer pool to reach out to simply doesn't exist.

2. Valuation variances

Different buyer's valuation opinions on the same business can vary greatly because of each buyer's post-closing strategy. For example, a buyer might have the ability to immediately cross sell the seller's customer base with theirs and/or have the ability to reduce 25% of the seller's operating expenses within 3-12 months post-closing ... while other buyers will only be able to reduce the seller's expenses by 5%. This enables one buyer to legitimately value the seller's company notably higher than other buyers. So it is a mistake to only think of the selling company when quantifying valuation, rather think of the logical buyer's post-closing strategies as well.

3. The #1 deal killer of all

As we know there are plenty of events and discoveries which can kill a divestiture. There is one discovery which stands out among the rest as being the #1 killer of all ... and that is when a seller lies about anything. If a seller lies about something irrelevant, and some do, certainly their incentive would be much higher to lie about something significant. Newly discovered seller dishonesty casts a vail of doubt on every piece of due diligence information the seller has provided. What used to surprise me is, this dishonesty would become apparent in cases where the seller's company was in great shape, growing and profitable. There was no reason to lie other than to get just a bit more money from a deal ... instead they end up paying a bit in the form of a reduced offer from the buyer (yet the seller sometimes doesn't realize it). On the other hand, I have seen distressed companies where at least the seller was honest about the miserable situation the company was in.

The mistake I have seen buyers make is to isolate the seller's dishonesty, as to think that the integrity pollution was contained to a single piece of due diligence information.

And the mistake I have seen sellers make is underestimating how smart and paranoid buyers are (... as they should be).

4. The importance of being extremely proactive in the first month of the divestiture process

The first mistake that some CEOs and business owners make is underestimating how proactive the divestiture process needs to be in the first month in order to maximize the final sale price. Think of almost any large fixed asset auction ... the more buyers at the auction ... the higher the final sale price. This is no different than selling a business. <u>The buyer pool must be identified, contacted and educated in a short period of time</u>. One of the reasons is, smart buyers will respond early with offers and the only way the CEO can know if that offer is the highest is to have identified, contacted, and educated the entire buyer pool.

Of course an offer deadline can be set where offers for the company are due 120 days from the start of the process, however this is really more logical and effective with public companies and much larger private deals >$50mm where the educational process is more on-site and involves the buyer's due diligence teams travelling back and forth from the target's many offices and engineering sites.

1. A weakness with bid deadlines is many buyers will wait until the final week, so for the prior weeks and months, the seller receives no real valuation feedback from buyers.

2. Some buyers might have already been looking at another target acquisition for a few months prior to knowing about this seller's company being for sale, and are not willing or able wait 120 more days for a deadline.

3. It should be noted that while I prefer not to have a bid deadline set, there is certainly a minimum time period after starting the process before early offers should be considered.

5. Acquisition targets are either growing fast and overpriced, or they are distressed

There is a misconception that most companies which are for sale are either growing fast and overpriced, or are in a distressed situation ... either way there are not many good deals out there. This is far from being the truth. I have had many sell side clients who are experiencing partnership disputes, divorces, health issues, the need for capital for another venture, retirement and other life scenarios where they are wanting to sell the company ... yet the company is not in trouble, it's doing just fine and is priced fairly.

6. Selling CEOs give too much credit to buyers needing to get funding

It is unfortunate how difficult it is to raise capital for acquisitions in the Internet service sector. Whether it is from a bank, an angel investor, a family office or a group of investors, the probability of a buyer raising capital in the Internet service sector is generally low. The problem is, too many buyers who have never raised capital for a company acquisition think they can and too many sellers believe these buyers.

In some cases, a buyer has borrowed capital in the past for a data center acquisition, yet later on is having trouble raising capital for another company acquisition because the value of the acquisition is far greater than the total value of the fixed assets being acquired ... as is the case with almost all SaaS providers, some cloud service providers, MSPs, & VARs.

When selling CEOs are comparing the best offers from buyers, it is a mistake to give too much credit to buyers who are going to need to raise the capital to fund the acquisition. It certainly doesn't help that some buyers know they are in the weak position, hence offer more favorable terms than other buyers to boost their position and secure the deal ... only to predictably renegotiate the deal downward at a future date.

What ends up happening is ...

1. The buyer's potential investors insist that the buyer go back to the seller and negotiate a better deal OR they will not provide the capital for the acquisition. <u>This renegotiation many times turns out to be worse than the #2 buyer's offer which was backed with "capital on hand" for the deal.</u>

2. The buyer cannot raise the capital.

3. After #1 or #2 occurs ... The other buyers that had the capital on hand for the deal have found another deal to acquire, or when re-approached by the selling CEO to pursue the deal for a second time, the buyer lowers their offer price and terms in fear that there must be something wrong with the seller's company.

Having said all of that, if there are no other options, give the buyer who needs to raise capital a chance ... some buyers actually pull it off.

7. Hearing back from buying CEOs or their M&A decision makers

Getting right to the point ... if I reach out to 100 CEO's (or their M&A decision makers) presenting each of them with a sell side client of mine, a far greater percent of these CEOs will return my message ... than if my sell side clients contact the same 100 CEOs themselves.

The reason is simple. Many of these CEOs would like to have an open line of communication with M&A professionals in the industry they are in ... and they would prefer not to hear a recurring sales pitch from the CEO of a company they are not interested in acquiring.

8. The Geography Equation

I catch myself on a regular basis with the misconception that a buyer for a certain company must be in a certain geographic location around the world.

Geography is especially complicated because with each deal, the following components of geography must be analyzed.

Which is more important for a specific deal?

- The countries the buying company's owners/investors live in?
- The countries the selling company's owners/investors live in? (absolutely important)

- The countries the selling and buying company's management and employees in?

- The countries the selling and buying company's customers in?

- The countries the selling and buying company's infrastructure in? Should there be overlap or would the value of the deal be much higher if there wasn't geographic overlap?

9. Manpower

There is a misconception with some selling CEOs that a proper divestiture strategy can be executed with someone in-house.

Managing a company divestiture is a full-time job. Yes, in some cases there is someone in-house who is capable of the job and has the time to devote themselves to the process, however; in most cases there isn't. Many times a mistake would be to force the CFO into this role. I don't know many CFO's with an extra 6-8 hours a day for the next 3-4 months.

The job includes assisting with the development of the divestiture strategy, the identification of the buyer pool (an ongoing process), the communication and education of each of the 50-300 prospective buyers (extremely time consuming), conference calls, document creation, negotiation, pre- and post-closing strategy.

Regarding the communication and education of each of the buying prospects … each time a prospective buyer is contacted <u>the communication needs to be documented</u>. This includes the original communication of the blind teaser, the response to that message, the NDA, the initial deck (Company

Overview & Financials), follow up documents (FAQ, engineering docs, vendor, customer and employee agreements), conference calls, managing offers ... on and on.

10. Deal exposure

While there are many well-constructed business brokerage web sites, one of the problems is not enough strategic buyers look at them ... and many sellers don't want their deal added to these sites. What I have found is a far greater % of financial type buyers than strategic buyers look at these business brokerage sites in the IT space. <u>While financial type buyers are always on the hunt for an investment, strategic buyers tend to be focused on running their companies when they first learn about an acquisition opportunity.</u> I don't want to take anything away from the value of these sites, because they are valuable tools for both the divestiture process and for finding a business, it's just a mistake to rely solely on these sites.

For every qualified buyer who responds to a sell side listing I place on one of the business brokerage web sites, I find at least 20-25 interested and qualified buyers by proactively identifying then contacting logical strategic buyers myself.

11. Divestiture strategy pivot

As the weeks pass, both the business owner (CEO), and the M&A professional learn from the feedback they receive from buyers. All feedback is important both the good and the bad especially if the same issue is continually brought to the forefront. Sometimes there is the ability to correct the negative issue during this process, and other times there isn't, rather just the opportunity to explain it in more detail. The issues which come up can be regulatory, certain asset valuations, legal, the seller's deal structure requirements not being met, on and on.

A divestiture strategy pivot could be in many forms so it is important to slow down and not get caught up in the momentum to get a deal done.

It is a misconception that a divestiture strategy pivot is a negative thing or diminishes value in some way. In most cases it does not, rather the seller was simply asking buyers to value a certain asset too much and that made the entire deal overvalued. In this case, the strategy pivot would be for the seller to keep ownership of the asset and if need be, lease the asset to the buyer post-closing.

… or the seller insisted on a certain deal structure which no buyer would agree upon. In this case, the seller needs to adjust the deal structure requirement and re-educate the buyer pool.

Whatever the divestiture strategy pivot is, make sure to think if you should take a step back and <u>re-identify the prospective buyer pool</u> which might be interested in the new divestiture strategy.

12. The trickiest type of Internet service company to market for sale

There is no doubt the trickiest Internet service company to market is one of the 1,001 flavors of a SaaS provider. This is primarily due to two reasons.

First, the buyer could be anywhere in the world. Second, the buyer could be from multiple industries depending upon which business function and vertical the SaaS is focused in.

The misconception I have seen many sellers possess is to restrict their scope of the buyer pool, insisting that the buyer must be in a single industry (or location).

When identifying the buyer pool during the initial phases of the divestiture process, as opposed to casting a wide net to include the world ... there are logical pockets of focus around the world depending upon the SaaS industry ... for example gaming in northern Europe and eastern Asia could never be ignored, and financial services in NYC, London and Frankfurt.

I find myself concluding over and over that regardless which industry my sell side client is in ... I make sure to include a buyer search in the major hubs of Internet innovation and finance ... San Francisco, NYC, Seattle, Boston, LA, Chicago, Austin, London, Toronto, Sydney ... and of course there are plenty of 2nd tier markets.

13. Outsiders can be longshots

This topic is taken from one of my previously written articles, but fits nicely into this "misconceptions/mistakes" article. From my experience "outsiders", who are buyers not presently in the same industry as the target company they are looking at, close far less deals as a percent of the deals they look at than industry "insiders". Here are the two main reasons:

1. This buyer is probably going to do two very smart things ... be paranoid and take their time. In analyzing this deal this buyer has a lot to do over the next few weeks & months. They have to learn about the industry, learn where my sell

side client's company ranks within the industry, quantify the pros and cons of each of the value drivers of my client's company, then come up with a valuation and proposed deal structure. Not only are they going to take way too much of everyone's time to come to a valuation and offer conclusion but <u>much of that time is likely to be spent obsessing about the wrong things</u>. The problem with their own diligence is they are competing against buyers who are already in this industry, buyers who under-stand the inner workings of all of the value drivers ... hence "insiders" move through the analysis process to the valuation and offer stage much faster.

2. The outsider cannot realize cost savings and other synergies which make a higher company valuation logical, so the outsider will almost never be the highest bidder ... and if they happen to be, the completion risk (from LOI to closing) is uncomfortably high.

So, the mistake here would be for a selling CEO to assume that when comparing offers from two buyers, one being an insider and the other being an outsider ... that they are both equally likely to close the deal.

14. *Billion-dollar buyers and million-dollar sellers*

It is a misconception by many business sellers that billion-dollar companies don't acquire tiny million-dollar companies. This is far from the truth. I have sold several sub $5mm private companies to multi-billion dollar publicly traded companies. Here are the reasons and logic why they do it on a regular basis.

Billion-dollar public companies don't make tiny million-dollar acquisitions then put out a news release expecting a positive reaction from the stock market. The truth is, knowledge of these tiny acquisitions is rarely made public because the actual company acquisition wasn't the strategy, only a part of it.

One way to look at the logic of a small private company acquisition is ... every billion-dollar corporation has salespeople right? ... and every time a salesperson makes an individual sale that sale doesn't "move the needle", yet it makes perfect sense for each salesperson to pursue individual customer sales. So, in many cases it's quite logical for a small team of managers to pursue strategic acquisitions and acquire 30,000 SMB customers with each deal ... even if each acquisition accounts for less than 1% of total revenue for the buying corporation.

There are many other reasons small private company acquisitions make sense yet "don't move the needle" such as:

- Faster entry into a new geographic market
- To acquire a new product or service offering as opposed to developing it in-house
- To test cross selling different products into the acquired customer base, or sell the acquired company's products/services back into the corporation's customer base
- Acquire a company's IP (Intellectual Property)

- Remove a competitor from a specific market

- Vertically integrate

- To do an "Acqui-Hire". For example, to acquire a small cohesive development/engineering team as opposed to attempting to hire them one by one.

- To continually train and give experience to the company's merger and acquisition team members: including managers from the legal, accounting, operational, sales/marketing and technical departments

- Maybe to practice a certain M&A strategy on a tiny deal in preparation for an upcoming much larger company acquisition where the cost of mistakes would be far greater

- To acquire a government issued permit or wireless license which a target company owns and it is cheaper and faster to acquire this company as opposed to going through the approval process. Or, there is an exclusive allocation issue where the target company acquisition is the only way to acquire the permit or license.

FOURTEEN

Software developers and architects ... "If you build it, they will come."

There are some cases when this expression is predictably accurate. For example, if you build a beer tent at a music festival ... they will come. Of course, there are a few other no-brainer examples of this but I want to address the other 98% of the economy.

People rarely say this expression out loud before something is built, rather they say it sarcastically when they are pointing out a failed business due to the then obvious lack of customer demand. Yet many entrepreneurs have this inner voice that whispers, "if I build it, they will come", over and over as their excitement about a new project grows.

Software developers and architects are a lot alike, both are creative engineer types. They have the ability to <u>practice</u> designing many projects inexpensively, without third party permissions or the cost of failure. In fact, it's better than that ... it's fun, therapeutic, thought provoking and a creative outlet ... similar to what musicians, writers, and painters experience. However, a big difference between software developers and architects is that a software developer can easily move a project to the next phase because it requires no 3rd party permission and very little capital to move forward. It's too easy to keep tossing a few thousand dollars in to keep the project moving from dream to reality.

On the other hand before architects can move a project from the drawing board to breaking ground, profit motivated third-party investors and lenders must get involved and be sold on the idea … not to mention receiving governmental approvals etc. <u>These third parties must be sold on the economic viability of the entire plan up until and years past "opening day".</u> Worded another way, not many architects would spend $500k of their own money starting to build an office complex which is going to require $4 million to complete without the other $3.5 million of funding in place … yet software developers do this all the time.

I receive calls almost every week from people who started to build a software product and hired a few people with the hope of the product evolving into the "<u>the most valuable of all Internet service businesses</u>" … a scalable SaaS! … yet are having difficulty signing up customers (primarily due to a lack of capital … and sales/marketing prowess) and having difficulty raising additional capital. The point of the call to me is to inquire about either raising additional capital (which I do not do), or selling the product "as is".

The problem with selling pre-revenue software dev projects/ businesses is, the prospective buyer pool for basically just the IP is so small. At best there are only a handful of existing entities already in the space or a closely related space which are willing to purchase it. What ends up happening is the software developer has way more invested in the development stage than any buyer is willing to pay them, so the developer "passes" on the initial offers from buyers. After time passes some of them go back to the buyers who made them offers only to find out that the original offer is no longer valid, or is valid but at a reduced price ... so nothing happens.

If you build it and they don't come, you will be in "no man's land" ... no revenue, no customers and no power to negotiate a profitable way out of the sunk development cost.

I don't want to finish this article with that less than cleaver reworked saying ... rather with the truthful statement that I have an enormous amount of respect for both software developers and architects. The frustration I have as an M&A professional is seeing so many projects come to a screeching halt because revenue was not able to be generated ... because there was never a viable funded marketing plan in place.

In closing, sometimes when a group of engineers looks at a group of sales and marketing types, they wonder with frustration ... "what the hell do they really do?" As a sales guy myself, I have been on the receiving end of "that look". The reality is those service widgets (as we called them in grad school) are not going to move themselves. We are a team, we need each other ... get more sales and marketing types involved earlier.

FIFTEEN

It's nice to meet you but you're an "outsider"

When I am selling an Internet service company most of my marketing efforts are proactive. I reach out to 100's of prospective buyers and investors who are already in the industry, or a closely related one. In addition, I am approached by prospective buyers wanting to look at my sell side client's company. My first glance at a buyer who approaches me is to determine if the company they represent is in the industry or a closely related one. If not, they are probably an "outsider".

Why this is usually a bad thing?

1. This buyer is probably going to do two very smart things ... be paranoid and take their time. In analyzing this deal this buyer has a lot to do over the next few weeks & months. They have to learn about the industry, learn where my client's company ranks within the industry, quantify the pros and cons of each of the value drivers of my client's company, then come up with a valuation and proposed deal structure. Not only are they going to take way too much of everyone's time to come to a valuation and offer conclusion but much of that time is likely to be spent obsessing about the wrong things.

The problem with their own diligence is they are competing against buyers who are already in this industry, buyers who understand the inner workings of all of the value drivers ... hence "insiders" move through the analysis process to the valuation and offer stage much faster.

2. The "outsider" cannot realize cost savings and other synergies which make a higher company valuation logical, so the "outsider" will almost never be the highest bidder ... and if they happen to be, the completion risk (from LOI to closing) is uncomfortably high.

Side Note: If the "outsider" does close the deal, the likelihood of the acquisition producing the originally forecasted ROI for their shareholders is much lower than an "insider" acquiring the same deal. In my opinion these "outsider" acquisitions make up a notable portion of the commonly thought <u>50% of M&A deals which end up being shareholder value destroying events.</u>

Moral of the story

It is safer for a buyer and their capital to "stay in their lane". Worded another way ... I would never invest my money in a private company acquisition in industries where I am an "outsider" ... such as hospitality, medical, manufacturing, construction, tourism, entertainment, energy, and a few other spaces ... why? because after spending 20 years in the Internet service industries, I realize that I don't know anything about how these other industries REALLY work ... and worse ... what if I end up being the highest bidder for one of these companies?

SIXTEEN

When there is no doubt it's time to sell your company

There are two stories I am told almost every week by Internet service company owners.

The first story is describing the situation where the business owner is making too much money each year to sell it, pay taxes, reinvest the proceeds, pay taxes on that income ... then compare those after-tax proceeds with the amount they are currently making from the business. Many times the amount of money they are making (or the total value they are extracting including benefits) is 5-8+ times greater than the after-tax proceeds from selling the business then reinvesting.

So my response is "You should keep the company, yet if you need to back away from it, hire someone to run it for you."

Side Note: There are many life scenarios which negate the difference in the two income comparisons above such as simply wanting to retire, divorce, poor health, need the capital for 101 reasons, and partnership disputes.

The second story is describing the situation where the business owner has partners and they have been disagreeing for years now, but it wasn't always like that. When the partners created the company they were smiling, laughing, "high 5-ing", dreaming, and working until midnight over and over. They put their hobbies aside, couldn't stop working, and couldn't be happier.

Similar to what happens with many band members in the music industry … over the years love evolves into hate. Days are absent of creativity and collaboration, yet are filled with anger and avoidance. Each partner's decisions are about "me" … not about "us".

This is no way to run a business, and no way to live a happy life.

Too often there isn't a partner who is right and a partner who is wrong, rather they simply want to steer the company in different directions … and they're both right.

So my response to all of the partners is … "Sell the business, go your separate ways … then maybe reconnect later in life … hug it out, laugh, and share your respect for each other for what you all achieved many years ago … together."

SEVENTEEN

Why billion-dollar companies acquire tiny million-dollar companies everyday

Over the last three months I have sold two small private Internet service companies (sub $5mm deals) to publicly traded companies which are valued at over $2 billion each. The point of this article is to discuss a common M&A myth that very large companies don't acquire very small companies. Some people believe that since a $3 million private company acquisition will simply not "move the needle" for a billion-dollar company because adding $1-5 million in annual revenue is less than ½ of 1% of total revenue of the buying company ... they won't do it.

Billion-dollar public companies don't make tiny million-dollar acquisitions then put out a news release expecting a positive reaction from the stock market. The truth is, knowledge of these tiny acquisitions is rarely made public because the actual company acquisition wasn't the strategy, only a part of it.

One way to look at the logic of a small private company acquisition is ... every billion-dollar corporation has salespeople right? ... and every time a salesperson makes an individual sale that sale doesn't "move the needle", yet it makes perfect sense for each salesperson to pursue individual customer sales. So in many cases it's quite logical for a small team of managers to pursue strategic acquisitions and acquire 30,000 SMB customers with each deal ... even if each acquisition accounts for less than 1% of total revenue for the buying corporation.

There are many other reasons small private company acquisitions make sense yet "don't move the needle" such as:

- Faster entry into a new geographic market.

- To acquire a new product or service offering as opposed to developing it in-house

- To test cross selling different products into the acquired customer base, or sell the acquired company's products/services back into the corporation's customer base.

- Acquire a company's IP (Intellectual Property)

- Remove a competitor from a specific market.

- To do an "Acqui-Hire". For example, to acquire a small cohesive development/engineering team as opposed to attempting to hire them one by one.

- To continually train and give experience to the company's merger and acquisition team members: including managers from the accounting, legal, operational, sales/marketing and technical departments.

- Maybe to practice a certain M&A strategy on a tiny deal in preparation for an upcoming much larger company acquisition where the cost of mistakes would be far greater.

- Vertically integrate

- To acquire a government issued permit or license which a target company owns, and it is cheaper and faster to acquire this company as opposed to going through the approval process. Or, there is an exclusive allocation issue where the target company acquisition is the only way to acquire the permit or license.

I am asked by business owners all the time ... "How do you even make contact with the CEOs of large public companies? They are impossible to reach."

I have been focused on private company M&A in the IT space for over 20 years ... and two very important processes I have learned are the totally different methods of communicating a company acquisition opportunity to a large public company verses a small private company CEO.

EIGHTEEN

A perfectly overpriced, initial "business asking price"

Most business owners like to start the divestiture process with an inflated asking price ... and unless it's totally outrageous, I go with it. Am I just being a nice person, or do I have an ulterior motive?

Of course I am up to something, but it's not that sneaky. Let me explain.

"Perfectly overpriced" means the asking price is ...

1. high enough that <u>no buyer will say</u> ... "ok Eric, we are willing to pay your seller what he is asking". So what does this accomplish? It shows the seller (and me) that buyers are not going to pay the dream price. Some sellers need to hear "your price is too high", from real buyers not just me.

2. high enough that it communicates to low ballers that this is not their deal. (I can always track them down later if need be).

3. high enough that I will have enough time to proactively identify, communicate with, and

educate a proper size pool of prospective buyers ... before the seller lowers the asking price and a few buyers start to talk about making offers. It can be very distracting to everyone on the seller's side when buyers start to express interest in making offers. It is such a natural complement to the seller's achievement, it's hard for them to resist engaging. <u>Sometimes the seller's focus turns to what these initial buyers are looking for, and away from the education that needs to continue to occur with the larger pool of prospects.</u>

Side Note: To give credit where credit is due. It is a smart buying strategy for a buyer to quickly learn about a business in their industry which is new to the market, get to know the seller and try to make a deal happen before other buyers do the same thing. There are plenty of buyers who understand this ... hence my race to get the word out about my sell side clients to at least 90% of the prospect pool before the smart buyers do this.

4. yet not overpriced to the point that buyers doubt our understanding of the market and/or the seller's honest intention to divest the company.

It should be noted there are occasions when the divestiture process needs to be expedited, (divorce, sickness, partnership dispute, lawsuit, tax issue, etc.), so the asking price is very attractive to buyers on Day 1 of the divestiture process.

Ineffective Buyer Strategy #1: Acting offended and/or losing interest in a deal because of the initial asking price.

When a buyer learns of seller's asking price and thinks the price is so high that it doesn't warrant more of their time ... they should first thank the seller, then ask to be sent a quick note in the future if the price is reduced.

The buyer's response <u>should not be</u>:

"Am I missing something? Your company is not worth anywhere near what you are asking. I am not interested.", or the 101 other less than diplomatic responses.

Does this buyer not have one minute, one month later to read an email from the seller stating that the asking price has been reduced? Some buyers forget that while the initial price is known ... <u>no one knows how soon, fast and far the asking price will drop</u>. (not even many of the sellers themselves)

Besides, even if the buyer doesn't get this deal ... real market deal pricing and structure information doesn't get much better than this. The buyer can get an accurate feel for the value that the pool of buyers eventually decided the company was worth. If a buyer cuts off communication following the day they hear the initial asking price ... <u>the value of the interaction is lost</u>.

Ineffective Buyer Strategy #2: Not even making an offer.

Buyers and sellers ... and yes I say silly things sometimes. One of my favorites is from buyers when they say ...

"I am not making an offer because I don't want to get into a bidding war with other buyers".

What the hell does that mean?

I sometimes share the thoughts ...

- Would this buyer prefer to only bid on companies that no other buyers are bidding on ... because no one else wants it, at any price?

- Is sending one offer in, considered "getting into a bidding war"?

- What about sending in the offer they were thinking of before they heard there were other bidders? Why is this now a bad strategy?

- Is there a strange fear of getting exactly what they want, for the price they were willing to pay?

This statement (avoiding a bidding war) used to puzzle me in a humorous way, but I soon realized that buyers who say this are simply not interested at any price over a low-ball offer, yet for some reason that statement seems to be the right thing to say at that time.

A perspective on "Overpaying"

Just because there are other bidders for a company doesn't mean the winner will have overpaid. From what I have seen, in many cases a company which was not looking for an acquisition, yet when presented with an opportunity in their industry, will make an offer with the following mindset ...

"We don't need it, but if we can get it cheap enough then we'll buy it … so here is our offer."

So this buyer is obviously not going to push the price up high.

Or other offers have a variable within the proposed deal structure that is unacceptable to the seller … so while this offer might be the highest monetarily, it is rejected by the seller.

So in the end, a reasonable offer with normal deal terms is many times the winner.

On the other hand, 0% might be right.

A common statistic regarding mergers and acquisitions across many industries is … 50% of all mergers and acquisitions were shareholder value destroying events. I have thought about this statistic for many years … as I have experienced then judged good and bad deals … wondering if 50% is too high or too low … and I keep concluding that 50% is about right.

50% may sound like a brutally high number, to the point that you wonder why anyone would consider acquiring another business. This is, until you compare it to the % of startups that fail every year and send angel investor's capital to heaven.

So doesn't this mean that the other 50% of M&A deals were shareholder value creating events? So in this 50% of the cases, the buyer didn't overpay … right?

Price is not the only measure …

Keep in mind, it's not always the price alone that eventually qualifies a deal a "shareholder value destroyer". Many times it is the buyer's post-closing strategy (a bad customer migration for example) that was so poorly executed ... <u>even if the purchase price was 20% less, the deal would have been a loser ... hence destroying shareholder value.</u>

In Closing

Many sellers have an ever changing emotional vs. analytical relationship with their asking price. In addition, there are shareholders, stakeholders, attorneys, accountants and family members giving them advice and pressuring them one way or another. It takes time for the seller to sift the noise and bias from reality.

The more that buyers understand this common phenomenon, and are patient with sellers ... the more successful their acquisition strategies will be.

NINETEEN

Never do business with this person

Of course I keep a list of the shady people I have met in the 20+ years I have been doing mergers and acquisitions in the Internet industry. The reason I maintain this "Never do business with this person" list is obvious, but there are other aspects of the list that are valuable yet maybe not immediately obvious.

Every day I meet new people from around the world. Most of them are honest with genuine intentions. As I get to know some of them I think to myself ... "if I needed to hire someone with those skills, I would love to work with them on a regular basis".

On the other side of the ethical spectrum ...

About 1-3 times per year, warning signs appear and I think I just might have a new addition to the list. Sure, I might be hypersensitive to this but it's my job. When I work for buyers I am supposed to sniff out fraudulent sellers, and when I work for sellers it is my job to keep crooks from getting in the way of legitimate buyers.

(A not so commonly known fact: Crooks on the buyside can cause just as much chaos as a crooked business seller.)

I am not quick to add someone to the list, but when I do, there is no doubt in my mind they belong there. In almost every instance I lose sleep as I access damage control and plan the escape from this "Satan in a suit".

What information is on the list?

Other than their name, I include the company, the other parties in the transaction, what they attempted to do (or were successful in doing), what the costs were, if there were warning signs, who else on their side probably knew about it, and any other highlights. And I of course keep all of the germane emails I can gather.

Updates

A few years ago I started to update the list from time to time because I want to keep up with these people ... not because I am going to reach out to them, rather I just want to know where they pop back up, because they almost always do. So I update the list by adding the name of their new venture or who they work for now, what city/country they are supposedly working in, what role they are assuming and any other highlights. Some of them disappear for years then pop up running a new company ... or as a senior/middle manager of a private company ... or in a country few people ever want to visit ... no doubt running from something.

Unlike working in many other industries where someone can move a few hundred miles away, replicate their unethical ways and go unnoticed for a period of time ... working in one of the many Internet service sectors anywhere in the world, is in many ways similar to working across the street from what they were running from. It is simply hard to hide.

So who else sees my list other than me?

No one else sees the list with all of the associated notes, but I do share some of the names with a very short list of other M&A professionals around the world who I have known for many years ... and they share names with me. <u>This collaboration has saved many people an enormous amount of grief, and money.</u>

Does anyone ever come off the list?

Absolutely not. Because, I don't have the patience for it ... and it's too risky.

So who makes the list, and who doesn't?

- Do buyers who took advantage of a desperate and/or uneducated seller make the list? ... No

- Do sellers who sold a near bankrupt company which everyone knew was a complete financial and operational mess, make the list? ... No

- Do buyers who are rude, classless, boiler room, hammer closing, "expert" bullies, make the list? ... No

- Do people who appear bi-polar, schizophrenic or have substance abuse issues and make terrible decisions as a result, make the list? ... maybe (It's a case by case basis.)

People make it to the list when they deliberately set out to steal from someone else, whether they were buying or selling a company (or assets). In my opinion, "stealing" is easy to define, identify ... and never forget. The definition doesn't need calibrating, it's consistent across industries, and it doesn't weather with time.

TWENTY

There are 4 company valuations for every Internet service company

I have been discussing Internet service company valuations for over 20 years and what I realized a long time ago is there are 4 valuations for almost every Internet service company.

1. There is the valuation that the company CEO/owner has in their mind.

2. There is my valuation opinion ... which other than deciding if I will accept the sell side assignment, is not very important because I am neither the seller nor the buyer.

3. There is the valuation range that most prospective buyers will come up with.

4. There is the valuation that the top 1-3 most logical and synergistic buyers will come up with as they discuss the seller's company behind closed doors.

While valuation #1 above might be a financial requirement for the CEO ... #3 & #4 are the only realities in terms of a transaction occurring. Focusing on receiving valuation #4 is the key to all successful company merger and divestiture strategies. <u>The steps to receiving valuation #4 are to identify, engage and educate the greatest number of logical buyers.</u>

Side Note: The guaranteed way to receive a low offer for the company is for a CEO/owner to only approach the easiest 1-2 buyers and force a sale to one of them ... yet business owners do this all the time. Why do they do this? Because they are either uncomfortable with the divestiture process, not aware that there are far more buyers interested in acquiring their company than the 1-2 buyers who approached them first, and/or they don't want to send a signal to the market that their company is for sale (even though there are ways to minimize this).

Identifying the logical buyers is only one of the hurdles, <u>communicating one on one with the corporate M&A strategy decision maker at each of these acquiring companies is the next hurdle</u>.

So who is the real M&A strategy decision maker at a tech company? ... who has the power within the company to actually make the company acquisition decision?

Many times I reach out to 4 or 5 of the top strategy decision makers at each company to make sure I reach the true power center of the company ... <u>and to increase the probability that an in-house conversation about my sell side client's company occurs</u>. Of course typically the main strategy decision makers are the CEO, President and Chairman but sometimes in the technology space the founder of the company chooses to sit back from the spotlight in the CTO/CIO/CSO role ... so I make sure to engage them as well.

Back to the highest valuation

When valuing a company, we all place greater or less emphasis on each of the typical variables such as: revenue, profit, customer base quality/growth/trends, fixed assets, IP, product/service strategies, management, employees, vendor relationships, on and on. Similar to conversations regarding religion or politics, one person rarely changes another person's valuation opinion very much, especially if they are on the other side of the negotiating table. But what is missing from many valuation conversations is the aspect of the value from the buyer's perspective. The value for the buyer depends on what that specific buyer is going to do with the company post-closing … <u>and many times this is unknown to the seller</u>.

<u>In many industries, not all, the same business can logically be worth a 100% greater valuation to some buyers than others</u> … so while there are always a few "low ballers" in the buyer pool, most buyers can be correct in their valuation opinion yet be far apart from the top 1-3 bidders.

In closing, it is in the seller's best interest to identify the greatest number of potential buyers, educate them, be polite to the low ballers, follow up with the runner ups to ensure understanding, and respect the #1-3 bidder's time.

TWENTY-ONE

Business liquidity/desirability scoring system

In the private merger and acquisition world, business liquidity and business desirability are most often highly correlated, so for this article I will use "desirability" because it makes more sense when we are looking at this through the eyes of a business acquirer.

I will present a very simple scoring system to illustrate the "desirability" of a private Internet service company. The scoring system is a casual way for me to present the different variables most business buyers initially look at, and for me to add more emphasis to some of them. While this discussion can apply to over 25 Internet service industries, the obvious imperfection with such a scoring system is each industry has its quirks and gems so one scoring model may never "fit like a glove" with every industry.

As a business owner reads each variable and realizes their company might receive a negative mark for that variable ... they might want to ask themselves the following ...

- is it possible to fix or improve this desirability issue before a company sale? If so, how much time and capital would it require?

- how will it affect the deal structure?

- how much will buyers discount the company valuation for this desirability issue?

- if buyers will discount the company valuation, is the discount less than the cost of fixing the issue before a sale.

It is also important for a first-time business seller to understand these concepts because in doing so the business owner is more likely to pursue the divestiture communication process with the appropriate amount of bravado. Worded another way, a business owner of an illiquid company might convey too much pride thus quickly killing a possible divestiture with the very few realistic buyers … while too sheepish a communication strategy with a very liquid company can lead to leaving too much money on the table.

These are the initial variables that most Internet service business buyers have in mind when they are sorting through the many businesses that are for sale on any given day, with a few of my comments about each one. (in no particular order)

- One-time revenue vs. recurring revenue: Recurring revenue is almost always more desirable than one-time revenue. (Give 1 point if the recurring revenue is greater than 25% of total annual revenue, 2 points if the recurring revenue is greater than 50% of the total revenue, 3 points for above 75%, 4 points for above 90%)

- Age of industry: There tends to be more buyers for the newly created service industries. (For an industry which didn't exist 5 years ago add 1 point. Take a point away if the industry existed 15 years ago.)

- Pre-revenue vs. revenue but not profitable vs. profitable: This category is the biggest wildcard in the article. We have all seen some pre-revenue companies being worth hundreds of millions, and some profitable businesses almost unsellable. Of course in most cases the profitable business is more desirable. (So, for profitable +2, revenue but not profitable 0, and pre-revenue -2)

- Portable: If the business can be moved then operated successfully in another city or country without a major expense, increased customer loss, or employee flight, then the business is portable and more desirable to most buyers. (Easily portable +2, it could be portable yet with a notable expense and some employee loss +1, it isn't portable -1)

- Owner is crucial to operations: Buyers want to know what will happen to customer churn, employee retention, and vendor relations once the owner leaves the company post-closing. (Is the departure insignificant +1, hard to tell 0, significant -3)

- Is the owner wanting to stay with the buyer's company or leave post-closing: It sure makes a buyer feel good if the owner prefers to stay with the company post-closing ... and really good if the owner is willing to take stock as part of the deal structure. Most owners want all cash and have something else to do with their life after the sale ... so this isn't a negative. Let's realize that most business founders become terribly frustrated with the way their business buyer operates their business post-closing and tend to leave 6-18 months post-closing even if they originally planned to stay much longer. (If the owner would like to stay with the buyer post-closing and take some of their stock as part of the deal +2, if the owner is willing to take some of the buyer's stock, but will not be able to stay with the buyer post-closing +1, if the owner needs all cash and will not be able to stay with the company post-closing -0-.)

- Owner's track record of building and selling a company: Has the owner built and sold a company before? (If the answer is: "Yes" and they are willing to provide an intro/reference to the buyer(s) of their previous company(s) +1, if "No" -0-.

- Top 1, 2, 3 customers are too big: Self (If the top 3 customers account for less than 10% of total revenue +1, if the top 3 customers account for greater than 33% -1, greater than 66% -3). If the top 3 customers make up more than half of the company's total revenue, this isn't a deal killer, but it will negatively affect the deal structure for the seller to protect the client flight risk the buyer will be assuming.

- Revenue/Profit trends: There are a lot of scenarios here other than revenue & profit growing, flat, or declining but for this simple analysis: (For fast growing revenues and profit +2, slower growing +1, flat 0, and declining revenue and profit -4)

- Scalable: How large can the company realistically become and equally important, will the incremental cost of adding new customers fall rapidly as more and more customers sign up. (highly scalable +2, somewhat scalable 0, not very -2)

- Potential pool of customers: Is the potential pool of customers limited for some reason beyond the ability of the company to overcome? Two examples of this are if a business is limited geographically or to a small niche industry. (Unlimited +1, limited 0, very restricted -2)

- Potential pool of business buyers: Is the pool of potential business buyers realistically just 3-5 easily identifiable companies (for example government regulated companies or niche SaaS providers), or maybe 25-50 companies? Or is the potential pool of buyers 300+ companies in many countries (for example old school shared web hosting companies)? (For 300+ +2, for 25-50 buyers +1, for 3-5 buyers -1)

- Key employees are too key: If any single employee left the company the week after closing, would their departure have an impact on the following year sales? I realize this is near impossible to quantify ... but you "get it". So, potentially what %? (For 0% +1, for 5% -2, for 10% -3, for greater than 15% -5)

- Geographic layout of the operations: I am referring to the geographic location (Cities and Countries) of the owners, management, employees, fixed assets (data centers etc.), and the customers. This is a long conversation and the same answer could be a positive or a negative depending upon the industry. So the question is, does the geographic layout of the company make a lot of sense to most buyers in the specific industry the seller is in, or would most buyers get a puzzled look on their face then ask the seller "why is X located there?". (For a logical layout +1, for a layout that is not ideal -1, for a layout that is so unusual it will definitely be a major discussion point -3. Geographic layout may be the most important variable of all and should be one of the first topics in a buyer/seller Q&A. The reality is, in the eyes of most business buyers the geographic layout is either going to make the deal a +9 or a –9.)

- Is there Intellectual Property ("IP") which needs to be valued: Many times it is best to talk about the value of the IP early on because in many cases the difference in the seller's and buyer's perceived value will be so great it will be an immediate deal killer. (If there is no IP or if the IP is a tiny percent of the total value of the deal, even if there is a big difference in perceived value between the buyer and seller, the deal could still happen +1. If the IP is a large percentage of the total value of the deal, and there is a big gap in the perceived value –9 and "game over" ... unless the IP is removed from the deal or creatively structured into the deal.)

- Expected deal structure: Rarely are deals structured with all cash at closing. It is more common with sub $20mm private deals to receive 65-85% at closing then payments within 3-12 months. (If the seller is willing to take payments for the company over a period greater than 12 months and is ok with these payments being contingent on future revenue +5, if the seller is looking for 65-85% then the balance over 3-12 months +1, if the seller is only willing to take 100% cash at closing -3)

The value of the scoring system is actually not the exact number of points, rather it is just the awareness of the analysis of the negative marks and their effect on company liquidity, valuation and deal structure.

TWENTY-TWO

Losing your job due to a tech merger or acquisition.

If you hear that the company you work for is being acquired, of course the first things you want to find out are ... is it true, who is the buyer, when is the deal closing, what is the probability of the deal happening, and will the buyer want to keep me or not?

Let me share some thoughts on the first and last concern.

Is the company really being sold?

If employees ask the CEO/Owner if the company is being sold ... this is a real dilemma for the owner. Does the owner tell the truth ... or not?

If word gets out that the company is for sale, the best employees might start to leave the company. This employee departure might make the buyer of the company walk from the deal because part of the reason for the acquisition is the top quartile of the employee talent base. Or for whatever reason the deal doesn't close, the company is worse off due to employee departures.

Worst Case Scenario:

So let's say the company is being sold and the initial plan is that the buyer will not be needing your services. My advice is ... be the classiest person to ever lose their job. Why?

1. The owner of the company might be your best source of a personal and professional reference for the next job. Even better, the owner might know your next boss. Most owners feel deeply about their employees and will try to help the departing employees the best they can.

2. If the deal hasn't closed yet there is a chance the initial personnel decisions will change. This happens all the time, even after layoffs are announced. If you were a jerk about the news, then your fate will not likely change. However, if you received the news with great class, then your fate might change.

3. If you quickly find another job, plans might change and the old or new owner might want you back. This can be used as leverage either with the new boss or the old boss. When the dust settles there is a chance you will be better off than before the original announcement ... granted, not without a few nights of lost sleep.

4. Sometimes after a proposed deal is announced more employees leave the company than the owner and the acquirer thought in their original planning. This might open up spots for you to stay. Only time will tell if this plays out.

5. Sometimes there are situations where a select number of people will be needed post-closing, but only for a transition period (training/migration etc.). This can be a great opportunity for you to simultaneously work with the acquirer and look for a new job. Who knows, the buyer might be impressed with you and offer you a much better job than the one you find during the transition period ... and maybe better than the one you had prior to the deal.

6. If you plan to work in the tech industry for the foreseeable future anywhere in the world, you will run into many of the same people over and over, maybe including the owner and senior management of the company you are about to leave. Believe it or not people will remember how you took the news. <u>It's interesting how many people are looking for the tiniest of events or actions to label someone either a really good or a really bad person. Try not to give people, many of whom might barely know you, the opportunity to label you for life because of a justifiably negative reaction to life changing news</u>.

7. And last but not least ... why you should be the classiest person to ever lose their job ... Because you know the owner of a tech company didn't owe you nor could promise you a job for life, so be thankful for the opportunity you were given. Over the years I have been amazed at how many business owners almost killed their own company divestiture or lowered the value of their deal because the employees were not

going to be taken care of to the degree they were comfortable with.

For those individuals who think they are safe from a layoff.

If the deal has been announced, yet the layoffs haven't been announced, don't assume that just because you are the top sales rep or the most senior engineer that your job is safe. It's a fair assumption but not a great enough one that you should not consider other employment options. For example, some-times the buyer currently employs a full team of engineers and may be able to use a few of the more junior (inexpensive) engineers, but not the more senior (expensive) engineers. The same applies to the sales, marketing, accounting and operations departments.

In conclusion

If you are being laid off from your job due to a merger or acquisition, stay professional, be appreciative for the opportunity you were given, and look for another job … yet wait until the deal closes to truly learn your fate. The specifics of private mergers and acquisitions sometimes change daily, so even if it is true that you are losing your job … it might not be true next week.

And yes, I lost my corporate America job in 1996 due to a merger (which luckily I knew was coming) after working for 5 years for some of the greatest people I have met in the business world. We are still friends today.

So what did I do? Since I lived in a small town where there wasn't a "building block" type job available, I left and went to graduate school and have been working for myself ever since helping business owners acquire, divest and value Internet service businesses.

TWENTY-THREE

The startup strategy "pivot" … there is a hidden cost

The business strategy "pivot" is common with tech startups. Typically the startup's founder/CEO implements a "pivot" when the initial strategy of the startup isn't working out … so a different strategy is pursued. This short article is not referring to the scenario where a software development company is working on 5 projects then decides to "pivot" 1 of the 5 projects in their portfolio. Rather, I am referring to typical startups where there is one focus, one initial strategy that is clearly not working out and a strategy pivot is executed.

First a logical question. Why would a founder/CEO prefer to "pivot" as opposed to shutting the business down and creating a new startup AKA "reboot"? The most significant reason is, it is very difficult and time consuming to assemble a cohesive development, engineering and marketing team. Once this team is in place, it's almost magical, fragile even, and not to be messed with, so the pivot keeps this team intact (if they are lucky). Another problem with the reboot is, the post pivot strategy might be based on the existing company's IP (intellectual property), so a reboot of the company's equity ownership with the intent of using the same IP might not be possible (at least not inexpensively).

So why would it ever make sense to reboot as opposed to pivoting the startup?

I know of one very real reason ... the psychological weight of the sunk cost which will eventually cloud the financial analysis of a future transaction.

Scenario A: "The Pivot"

1. Investors contribute $1.5mm cash into hiring staff and development cost

2. then 6-18 months later the initial strategy is obviously not working out so they think of a slightly different strategy and pivot the company, and invest another $1mm cash into the company to proceed toward the new product/service strategy

3. then 2-3 years later they either want to raise capital by selling equity or sell the entire company. The problem is, if they find a buyer who offers $2mm (or values the company at $2mm for an equity investment), <u>the original investors could have the mindset that they have $2.5mm invested into the project and they are not likely to agree to the $2mm valuation, because that would be a loss</u>.

This "mindset" kills proposed transactions all the time, hence kills startups because later the original founders realize that the proposed $2mm offer was their only lifeline ... yet is no longer available. It is unfortunate in some cases because the post pivot strategy could have been "the next best thing", and all it needed was a little more growth capital and maybe that next level executive to step in and take the helm.

Scenario B: "The Re-Boot"

As opposed to pivoting the company, if they would have admitted "this idea didn't work" and closed the business (and maybe taken a tiny tax write off), they could have started a new company and only had $1mm cash invested into the new strategy ... then the $2mm buyout (or next round investment valuation) looks a lot better and would likely be accepted ... then the startup is off to the next level of growth.

You might be thinking ... if it's the same original investor(s), what does it matter if they pivot or re-boot ... it's the same money so why not pivot.

The psychology of investing is complicated. Over time investors get what is called "investment fatigue". As more and more time passes they contribute more and more cash into the startup, hence they become tired of the investment that hasn't yet paid off. With a business closure and a fresh start, the investment fatigue hasn't built up because the first business was written off as a loss ... financially and mentally.

I'm not suggesting the reboot is always the way to go, because more times than not the pivot is the smarter path for a startup because of the cohesive team in place. I just wanted to bring up this phenomenon as a discussion point for those decision makers who are contemplating a pivot.

TWENTY-FOUR

First discuss the geographic layout of the Internet service business with its owner

In the first hour with a prospective sell side client I need to learn a lot about the company and about the seller's style ... so I need to listen way more than I talk, respect the storyteller, ask the right questions, and manage the time we have.

The way NOT to spend this first hour is for me to quickly review the financials then open my mouth and blab like I know what's going on with this seller's business ... because sellers hate when people do that, and besides, financials many times disguise and distort what is really happening ... so I need to hear the story first.

Since most Internet service companies have owners, management, employees, customers and assets in many geographic locations around the world, I suggest in the first hour we discuss the location, history and set-up of all of the aforementioned human resources and fixed assets. This lengthy conversation inevitably reveals all sorts of intangibles I need to know in order to properly market and sell the company.

The geographic locations of each of these assets have huge implications on the liquidity and valuation of the company. Sometimes the geographic set-up enables a negative cash flow company to actually be sellable. Unfortunately the reverse is true as well, the geographic set-up can make a profitable company extremely illiquid ... as far as selling the company as a whole.

There are always buyers looking for a 2nd or 3rd customer support center halfway around the world so they can offer and advertise "in-house customer support 24/7" ... so why not acquire a company that already has one (even if it's presently losing money). There are 101 examples of this.

Once this "first overview" of the company is complete, I propose we review the financials because I then have an idea of what I am looking at ... and in the eyes of the business seller I am now "checked out" to make comments about their company.

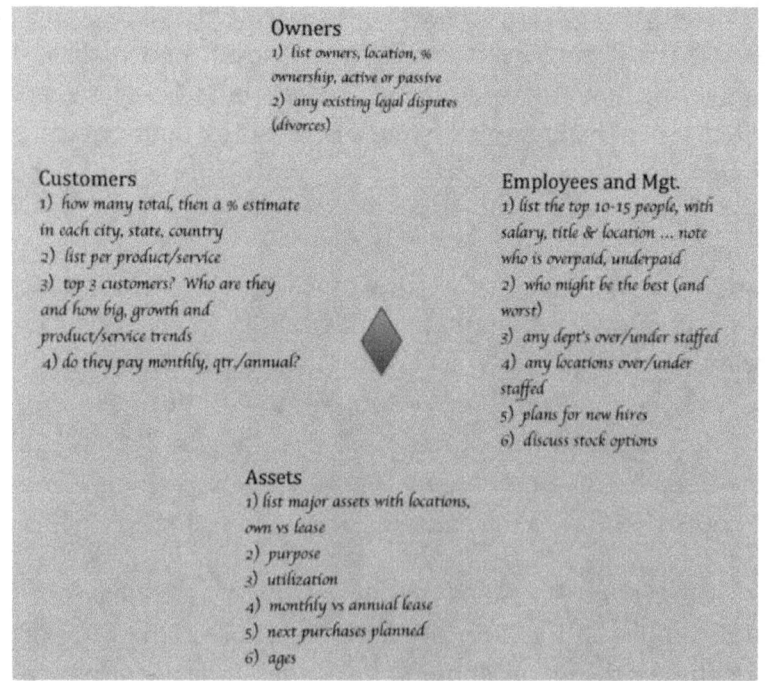

Side Note: The specific way I take notes during the exploration chat is what I call my "Geographic Diamond" ... but really it's just a large, messy doodle. I start discussing the ownership, then the employees, assets and finally the customers. Here is a sample of what I start with ... yet for the purpose of showing the reader what I am referring to I added a few of the questions I ask during the discussion to keep it going. (but of course we never make it thru all of these)

Once the initial discussion is over and I have made my way around the geographic diamond, my note taking pages are full of lists, arrows, pros and cons, additional questions and information requests ... THEN I review the financials with the business owner and have better questions to ask.

In my 20+ years of doing M&A, I have found the above exercise is a productive and respectful way to get to know a seller and their business.

TWENTY-FIVE

There is a better question to ask the business owner than, "Why do you want to sell your company?"

When business buyers have initial conversations with business owners who wish to sell their companies, one of the first questions is "Why do you want to sell your company". Over the years I have asked this question 100's of times. It just seems like a natural conversation starter, which it is.

However I came to the conclusion a few years ago that other than to see if this person is long winded or someone who gets to the point quickly ... the question and answer is rarely helpful. <u>It many times directs the owner to say something awkwardly positive about the company they really want to sell.</u> I almost always hear something irrelevant which never addressed the past, current or future state of the company ... so why keep asking this question when there are plenty of other questions to ask someone as a conversation starter.

What about ... "What are you going to do with your life after you sell your company?"

It may sound similar to the first question but the difference is ... this question is not about the company at all rather it's about the owner's life. <u>I feel better for my buyside clients if the owner immediately responds with some definitive life</u>

plan that can only happen after the company is sold. If the owner responds with a version of "I am not sure, no plans really", then I might be a little suspect that a deal will ever happen.

I have found that owners who have something big and exciting planned following the sale of their company typically have their companies priced reasonably and are more motivated to muscle their way through the entire divestiture process, than owners who have no plans at all. So if a buyer is looking at two very similar target companies to acquire, "all else being equal" I recommend initially pursuing the company where the owner has a grand plan for their life post-closing.

Finally, if you really want to ask the seller "Why do you want to sell your company?", go ahead and ask ... there is nothing offensive about the question ... however more times than not if the real answer has anything to do with the business, "the reason" is somewhere in due diligence ... and it's up to you to find it.

TWENTY-SIX

Positive thoughts for startups raising capital

Most angel investors are not like the crew on "Shark Tank".

Most angel investors ...

1. don't have unlimited funds (at least for speculation)

2. don't have (nor want) a team of business development and marketing managers who oversee all of the startups they invest in ... like the crew on Shark Tank

3. ARE looking for specific investments in industries they know very well. They are NOT willing to invest in 101 different industries they don't have experience in ... like the crew on Shark Tank does because a $250k investment is an irrelevant about of money to them ... and it's a TV show!

So the point is, when you present your startup to 100 angel investors (either in a group presentation or one by one over many months) ... don't take it personal when 98 of them are not interested, because most of them are looking for a niche investment opportunity that odds are you are not pursuing.

Having said that, when the other 2 of the 100 angel investors approaches you after your presentation and proceeds to tell you more about your startup than you knew yourself ... and they're still interested! ... resist the temptation to do a deal as fast as you can. This relationship can be as serious as getting married so slow down and think about who this person is, what their track record is and what this person can do for the startup other than just throw money in. Then go present to another 1,000 angels, virtually and face to face, because it might take that many.

Do yourself the favor of appreciating and recording the specific, positive and negative, yet free advice you hear from experienced angels, even if they don't invest ... that day ;-D

TWENTY-SEVEN

2 types of business sellers ... proud and desperate

This is a short writing for newer business buyers as opposed to the old veterans of the deal trail. After working M&A in the Internet service sector for over 20 years I have learned to respect the differences between all of the types of sellers that are out there. This writing is about <u>two of the extremes</u> ... the proud seller and the desperate seller.

What I have found is ...the total price most buyers pay for a company owned by the proud seller is more predictable than the total price most buyers <u>will eventually</u> pay for a company owned by the desperate seller. Let me explain.

Who are they?

Proud Sellers:

- They are so proud of their profitable and growing company they cannot stop talking about it.

- Every time I ask for a specific due diligence document, the seller provides it quickly and sometimes includes a verbal presentation. The document is thorough and many times provides more information than what I asked for.

- They try to grab every dollar in every aspect of the divestiture transaction ... as they have done with their vendors and customers for years ... (There is nothing wrong with that ... it's the reason their company is so profitable.)

- The proud seller has avoided lawsuits until this point and certainly doesn't want to deal with a lawsuit post-closing ... so a clean company divestiture is usually the result.

- These are the type of sellers that business buyers tend to build long term relationships with post-closing.

- The best employees typically want to stay with the company post-closing.

- The largest customers of the company are happy and have been adding business to their accounts in the trailing quarters and years.

- The buyer is likely to learn better ways to run a business in this industry.

Desperate Sellers:

- This seller is usually running a flat or declining company. This is sometimes slightly disguised by a single profitable division, one very large customer using multiple accounts and names, inaccurate financials or an unrelated business tucked into the company which the seller wants to keep post-closing.

- These sellers have been experiencing the daily stresses of the business downturn for many quarters if not years. Some sellers will be at their personal worst as far as ethical business practices.

- When I ask this seller for specific due diligence information, it takes too long to generate and is usually incomplete. What follows are the reasons that specific information cannot be provided.

- They realize most of the stakeholders in their company will be losers in the inevitable transaction(s). They also realize the only winners will be the buyers who acquire the pieces ... and sometimes they divert their resentment towards them.

- Some inexperienced buyers, especially those responsible for investing other people's money, get a little too excited to be investigating and bidding on a distressed company ... they are almost begging to complete a deal. Desperate sellers are hungry for this type of inexperienced buyer and will exploit this individual.

- The seller's desperation (and possible fraudulent behavior) will reach its peak before an actual bankruptcy ... the last-ditch effort to save the company and/or raise cash to divert to the original investor group (or just themselves). It is the buyer's responsibility to detect that a bankruptcy (or pre-bankruptcy implosion) is right around the corner. If the financial statements are not accurate, the imminent business implosion might not be obvious to the inexperienced buyer.

- When the deal is completed (and migrated) … buyers might end up with just the <u>slow paying & low margin customers, the least productive employees, angry vendors, an unwarranted bad reputation, lingering lenders, looming lawsuits, and less than impressed investors.</u>

Moral of the story

A buyer might be better off befriending the proud seller and acquiring their company, even at a premium, because accurately quantifying the total risk & eventual real return is extremely difficult with distressed business acquisitions.

TWENTY-EIGHT

7 things to do 13 months prior to selling your Internet service company

1. Organize the Profit & Loss Statements:

   Don't make the buyer's job of learning about the company difficult. 13 months out from selling your business is the perfect time to organize the P&L's, so in 13 months you can have a much improved "Trailing 12 Months P&L's" for buyers to look at. Buyers want to look at income statements which show as much detail as possible. For example with revenue categories as opposed to showing "Service Revenues", buyers want to know how much revenue is generated over time from each service the company offers. Of course buyers are going to want to know this and will ask for it so why not make the educational process easier. On the expense end of the P&L, as opposed to showing "Management Salaries", buyers want to see how much each manager earned. Why? because in many cases not every manager will be retained following an acquisition ... and the reality is, not every manager wants to stay following the acquisition. The same applies to each of the expense categories down to the basics such as

"Software Licenses". Of course buyers want to know how much is being spent each month for each software product.

There shouldn't be a long story associated with reading the financial statements for the first time. Typically the longer the story required to understand the financial statements as they relate to the current status of the business, the worse the situation is.

2. Organize the Balance Sheets:

Update the balance sheet each quarter, as opposed to just a single "Year End" version. Clean up the A/R, and remove, properly name and/or consolidate the personal items on the balance sheet. The balance sheet should be a story about the business, not a story about the founder's personal life.

3. Corporate Structure:

Meet with your attorney and accountant to review the tax implications under both a stock sale and an asset sale, and scenarios selling <50% and >50% of the company. Being 13 months out will give you time to make legal structure changes which could make a dramatic difference in the after-tax proceeds of the sale.

4. Non Core Assets:

Either sell these assets during the 13-month period (preferably sooner rather than later to show the non-effect of these assets on the business) ... or have a plan for the non-core assets if the buyer doesn't want or will not fully value them.

If your business is actually 2-3 businesses under one brand name sharing assets and personnel, this is the time to start cleaning up. This takes time and if not addressed properly, could delay the sale, reduce the value of the sale, or even prevent the sale from happening.

5. Disputes (legal or not):

   Settle and document all disputes with former/existing employees, vendors, customers, lenders, partners, etc. Unsettled disputes can prevent any merger or acquisition from occurring.

6. Focus on the core business:

   This is not the time to invest in a capital-intensive project which will not be positive cash flow for a few years. If a new product or service offering is pursued, great, just keep detailed accounting records on what was allocated to each new product/service in case you pull back from this you can attempt to get an adjustment with the buyer on these investments.

7. Prepare for your new life:

   This may sound silly but it has caused sellers problems before. They held up a sale because their next phase in life wasn't ready and they wanted to make the jump from one to the other.

TWENTY-NINE

The difficulties of selling a 50/50 equity partnership

When business partnerships are formed the obvious benefits and concerns are addressed.

- How do each partner's strengths and weaknesses complement each other?

- How much capital will each partner contribute to get the business going, and to keep it going until it reaches cash flow break even?

- How long will they grow the business until they entertain selling it?

Is that it? ... hardly.

As months and years pass, economic and industry variables will change which will affect the business. There are constant decisions with regards to the mixture of product and service offerings, and the decisions to get into other lines of business or get out of certain ones. There will be questions such as ... should the new focus be on a higher volume, lower profit margin business model or vice versa? What about a shift to a more capital-intensive model and less of a reseller model? On and on ...

If the business becomes a success, often times more capital is needed. Both partners need to agree on the investment proposal which includes who/where to get the capital from, how much capital to seek, how the capital infusion is structured and what to do with the capital.

And what if one of the partners wants to accept capital from a family member? This gives life to an entirely new set of concerns.

What if one of the partners personally acquires an asset for the business whether it's land, a building, a small data center, a thousand servers, or to complicate things further contributes intellectual property of some sort. When the company is to be sold, what is the value of the partner's contributed asset? Who is supposed to value it? These can become insurmountable hurdles.

Years later when it's time to sell the company the financial situation of each partner has no doubt changed since the company was founded. The consideration for the company could be all cash, all stock or a combination of both. The tax implications of each of these scenarios are probably different for each partner.

Moral of the story

Partners spend years growing the business then totally disagree about when to sell, who to sell to, how much to sell it for, and what the terms will be.

My suggestion ... one ship, one captain ... because in a two-equity partner business, one person has to be able to make these 100s of decisions without constant stalemates.

Don't start the company with a 50/50 split and don't let the equity division ever evolve into a 50/50 split.

About the Author

Michael Eric Furlow is President of Furlow Consulting, an Internet mergers, acquisitions and divestitures consultancy. He is a graduate of Bentley Graduate School of Business in Waltham, MA, earning a Master of Science degree in Finance. Following four wonderful years in the US Navy and a stint in corporate America as the Director of M&A at a wireless telecom company, Eric has been involved in over 250 technology-related transactions since 1996, assisting corporations & individuals around the world acquire, divest and value Internet service companies, such as web hosting, cloud services, IaaS, SaaS, eCommerce, VARs, MSPs, VoIP, digital agencies, and in the old days ISPs.

www.ingramcontent.com/pod-product-compliance
Lightning Source LLC
Chambersburg PA
CBHW050005230526
45465CB00003BB/1269